All the recipes

PASTA

of

ITALIAN CUISINE

DEMETRA

Editing: Monica Del Soldato

Layout: Margherita Sciarretta

Photography: Arc-en-ciel, Archivio Demetra

Translation: Helen Cleary and Helen Glave for Lexis, Florence

ALL THE RECIPES
PASTA OF ITALIAN CUISINE
1st edition July 1999
© DEMETRA S.r.l.
Via Strà, 167 - S.S. 11
37030 Colognola ai Colli (VR)
Tel. 045 6174111 - Fax 045 6174100

INTRODUCTION

ALL IN A SINGLE DISH

◆

Pasta represents the absolute corner stone of Italian cooking and that is why we have decided to dedicate an entire recipe book to some of the best-known Italian pasta dishes. We have selected some of the most celebrated regional dishes but also some original and tasty ideas and some suggestions which transcend regional boundaries.

If our baked lasagna is not exactly the one your Italian grandmother made, it might be the one made by the grandmother of your best friend. Each recipe, in fact, has many variants according to region, province, or the inspiration of the cook.

We hope that, rather than follow to the letter all the instructions given in the recipes, your own creativity will be stimulated to the point where you produce your own version, with secret ingredients which will distinguish it from all the others and make it special.

ITALY = PASTA

◆

The creation of pasta, understood as a cereal dough broken down with water, goes back a long way. There are traces in Etruscan bas-reliefs, and in Greek and Roman texts. What is certain is that dry pasta was consumed during the Arab domination of Southern Italy, long before Marco Polo came back from the Orient (1292) with his tales of Chinese Soya spaghetti.

Initially pasta had a simple form (*vermicelli* or *maccheroni, spaghetti, tagliatelle*) and it was only later that various more imaginative formats evolved. At the same time, the pasta was filled and transformed into *tortellini, ravioli, agnolotti*. The dough could also be modified to produce several types of *gnocchi*.

The first sauces were formed from spices, honey, milk or vegetables. Only with the great exploratory expeditions of 1500 did the tomato arrive in Europe (along with the aubergine, pepper etc.), but it was first thought to be a fruit with magic properties. It was the Sicilians who exploited it as a sauce and who sealed the classic match: 'pasta with tomato sauce'.

This brings us to the nineteenth century. Nino Romano writes: 'In 1800 the first pasta factories were founded. In Parma in 1811 tomato concentrate was produced, better known as 'black conserve'. [...] In 1835, in Boston, the first important factory for the production of bottles of tomato sauce was opened. In 1900, with the introduction of electrical energy, the production process was developed.' (*Le ore della pasta*, Ed. Acanthus).

Pasta has become a symbol for Italy all over the world and the three-coloured plate of spaghetti, tomato and basil is recognised everywhere as a message of joy and good cooking.

MEDITERRANEAN DIET, BALANCED DIET

◆

In the 1950's, with the economic boom and the advent of affluence, Italians abandoned traditional eating habits. To respond more closely to the image of 'humanity immersed in the frenetic rhythm of modern life' created by progress, the average Italian became increasingly attracted to the American eating style and shunned traditional dishes with their uncomfortable connotations of peasant life. Out went pasta, bread, rice; in came meat, pre-cooked and ready-to-eat foods and the colourful and super-filled sandwich. Italians, too, learned to eat on the run and they soon lost the habit of the midday meal, preferring a fast food snack in a café. Down with wine and water, up with fizzy drinks.

With progress came the so-called afflictions of affluence - heart problems, cholesterol, hypertension, arteriosclerosis, obesity etc. Science laid the blame on stress, on unnatural living rhythms, on a sudden change in lifestyle. The branch of science which studies nutrition principles, confirms the existence of a definite link between eating habits and bodily health.

To keep in good health you need to choose an eating style which is well-balanced and complete. The diet which incorporates these characteristics is the traditional, Mediterranean, Italian peasant diet which Italians themselves were inclined to eschew because it was considered old-fashioned.

It is advisable to avoid eating quickly, on the run, and to force yourself to find the time to sit down at a table to foods such as cereals, vegetables, fruit, fish, dairy products, vegetable oils and a little meat. The Mediterranean diet, as well as contributing to physical and mental health, is advantageous also from an economic point of view because costly ingredients can be avoided.

Pasta without gaining weight

◆

The principle of the Mediterranean diet does not consist exclusively of eating Italian products, but also of knowing how to select and to balance, combining the products in such a way as to give the body proper nutrition. In the last ten years aesthetic preference has been oriented increasingly towards an ideal of thin, long-legged, evanescent men and women. For someone with the Mediterranean physique, this can only be obtained at the cost of strict diets which ban pasta from the table. Apart from the futility of chasing a physical ideal imposed on us by advertising, eliminating some foods from our daily intake means threatening the health of our organism which needs a series of precious elements. Among these components, carbohydrates, present in a generous quantity (60%) in cereals, constitute one of our most important sources of energy.

If you have a real weight problem, or if you want to keep yourself fit, it is useless following a diet which is too strict. Often, in fact, kilos which are lost through hard sacrifice, come back on as soon as you go back to a normal diet. Apart from having a negative effect on our organism, this also influences our nervous system.

Robert Salvatori writes: 'The solution to being overweight is in our own hands; you only need to tackle the problem with common sense and determination.' (La Dieta Mediterranea, Idea Libri). It is not, then, by changing traditional eating habits that we keep fit but by following moderation and balance in our daily diet.

In particular, as regards the dishes in this manual, there are around 360 calories in 100 g of pasta, which is nothing if we consider that our daily requirement is 2,500-3,000 calories. It is sufficient to keep a check on the size of the portion, the sauce which goes with the pasta and the other foods that follow in the meal.

BALANCE AND MODERATION

◆

We have said that you should give your body all the elements it needs in the right quantity and to try to distribute carbohydrates, proteins, vitamins, mineral salts, fats, etc. over three daily meals (breakfast, lunch, dinner).

By including a plate of cereals in your menu, for example, you will supply your body with carbohydrates, mineral salts and enzymes (particularly if you use biological wholemeal pasta) which can be easily rounded off by a plate of vegetables, perhaps flavoured with extra virgin olive oil. The small proportion of protein (11% in the pasta) can be compensated with the addition of legumes, a little meat, fish or cheese. You will see then, that if you cook a first course with a sauce made of vegetables and other ingredients with protein, you will have a meal in a single dish which will satisfy your appetite as well as your bodily requirements.

The dishes of the Italian tradition, especially those with a pasta base, correspond to the criteria framing the re-evaluation of the Mediterranean diet. But it must be remembered that Italian tradition is principally a peasant one, and that its dishes were particularly substantial since they had to provide energy for prolonged physical activity.

The affluent society has reduced the amount of energy spent in a day: we don't move around much by bike, even less on foot and if we work, often we do so sitting down for many hours behind a desk or in a car and so on. We should therefore try to modify the quantity of some of the ingredients used in the preparation of the pasta dishes.

Progress has not been wholly negative: it has allowed us to get to know new products and to consider again those we had forgotten. This allows us, for example, to prepare a traditional lunch while skilfully avoiding, through substitution, the ingredients which we digest less easily and which are not so compatible with our bodies, without giving up the things which food represents: health and pleasure.

If sometimes you give way to your appetite, it's a good idea to follow (or precede) a sumptuous meal with a light snack, so as to spread out the work of the stomach and to allow it to digest the superfluous food. As for exercise, you should try to include a few stairs, climbed energetically, in your daily routine or else an hour's walk or the use of a bike to get to work etc. As well as a sense of well-being, a correct diet will reward you with a relaxed, fit body and an uncluttered mind.

APPROPRIATE SAUCE

As we have said, a plate of pasta does not greatly cut into our daily calorie allowance

(100 g dry pasta = 200-250 g cooked pasta = 360 calories). This does not authorise us to eat as much as we want: smaller portions, from 60 to 80 grams will allow us to follow a pasta dish with moderate portions of other foods which will give our bodies what we need without overdoing it.

Care must also be taken, however, in the use of sauces and added ingredients, to which the caloric value of the plate of pasta we want to eat is strictly related.

The substitution or reduction of a sauce is based on taste. On the next pages we have preferred to present recipes in their traditional version: you will find, for example, lard as well as butter. Try by yourself to substitute where possible with extra virgin olive oil, the cold-pressed type,(i.e. produced by mechanical olive pressing without chemical manipulation but only washing, sedimentation and filtration) which does not contain more than 1% or its weight in acidity (expressed in oleic acid). This type of oil provides a dressing which is rich in unsaturated fatty acids and, because of its chemical composition, is subject to only minor alterations in cooking which are not harmful. On the other hand, use frugally and with care, sauces and dressings based on animal fats: apart from being rich in saturated fats, butter, for example, when brought to a high temperature (200°C), becomes toxic.

FOOD COMBINATIONS

◆

In order that all foods, even those which are apparently lighter, do not become toxic, or difficult to digest and therefore bad for our metabolism, they should be combined correctly with the other components of our meal. The stomach does not secrete only one type of gastric juice but rather, the juice becomes 'personalised' according to the kind of foods it has to deal with. When we eat starch (rice, pasta, bread etc.), the stomach produces a gastric juice which is lightly acidic (neutral). When, on the other hand, we eat protein (meat, cheese, etc.) the digestive process requires a very strong enzyme activated by hydrochloric acid.

If not restricted to special occasions (the pleasure of transgression cannot be overlooked), incorrect food combinations can result in the fermentation and putrefaction of the food in the intestine, facilitating a series of digestive problems (headache, colitis etc.) as well as, in general terms, a weakened resistance to illness.

Since it is better to avoid the pasta plus meat combination (this can be transformed into a single dish and the following meal kept light to compensate), let's have a look at the ingredients which can be used with pasta.

- **Legumes:** the protein they contain supplements that contained in pasta, which is of a poorer quality and lacks some essential amino-acids.
- **Vegetables:** raw or cooked, they can be combined with pasta in large quantities. The only precautions should be taken with potatoes (also rich in starch), spinach and tomatoes (acidifying foods).
- **Fruit:** depends on the acidity and the maturity of the fruit. In any case this combination

requires caution and should only be used occasionally. The same applies to oily fruit.

• **Cheese:** avoid those which are low-fat and give preference to mature, slightly fatty cheeses.

• **Milk:** it is not easy to digest with pasta but can be used occasionally.

We wish to offer advice without turning you away from tasty preparations which might be in conflict with food combination principles. You simply need to go easy, without weighing down the stomach with starters or sweets, keeping servings small and helping the digestion with a little exercise after the meal.

PASTA: TYPES AND FORMS

◆

Pasta is simply the result of mixing water with flour obtained by the milling of wheat. There are two types of wheat: **durum wheat**, which, when milled produces *semola* and *semolato* and **common wheat** which, when milled, gives white flour.

Dry factory-made pasta produced industrially generally has a base of only durum wheat flour and this guarantees its durability, firmness when cooking and taste. Since durum wheat is more expensive, this is usually mixed with common wheat. Italian law guarantees that dry pasta in the shops cannot have more than 7% common wheat flour while foreign makes do not safeguard this characteristic in any way. It is easy, however, to identify the brands to avoid.

Good quality dry pasta can be recognised for its yellowish colour, its slightly sweet flavour and for the fact that it is odourless. It can be stored for a long time in a dry, dark place. Fresh pasta can be kept for less time (a few days) and should be kept in the fridge. The packets should be kept closed to protect from dust and insects.

Wholemeal pasta deserves a special mention. This is pasta which is factory-made and un-treated by refining processes. Refinement de-prives the flour of the wheat's natural proper-ties which makes it a balanced element: pro-tein, sugar, fats and mineral salts, vitamins and enzymes. Be careful, however, to choose only wholemeal pasta produced with cultivated wheat without the use of anti-mildew or other toxic products, which leave a residue on the grain of wheat.

Further care should be taken to choose a pasta actually produced with wholemeal flour and not simply with normal flour with the addi-tion of bran. The latter will not have a normal, uniform amber colour but rather a freckled appearance which reveals the presence of added bran.

Both regular and wholemeal pasta are found in the shops, and their different characteristics are shown on the labels.

- **Regular, dry pasta:** produced with durum wheat flour
- **Dry egg pasta:** this includes 200 g egg for each kilo of flour.
- **Special fresh or dry pasta:** this is made with flour and coloured with a percentage of spinach, desiccated or powdered tomato,

tomato concentrate or egg (200 g per kilogram of flour).

• **Special dry pasta:** produced with flour to which has been added a percentage of malt or gluten so as to increase the protein value to 15-20%.

• **Fresh pasta:** this can be produced with only durum wheat flour, only common wheat flour, a combination of both, and/or other ingredients.

There is also a range of diet pastas in the shops, for babies, diabetics etc. We advise you always to look for the trustworthy brands (which are not always the best known), when it is not possible to buy from hand-made pasta shops. Sometimes, for convenience, eggs or other added ingredients are substituted with chemical additives and colorants.

It seems that in Italy there are 500 formats of pasta and still today, producers follow whims of their imagination to create an increasing number of new types to tantalise the eyes and taste buds of the buying public. In general, the formats on sale can be grouped as follows:

• **Long, rounded pasta** with varying diameters: (*vermicelli, spaghettini*), and sometimes hollow (*bucatini, zite*).

• **Long narrow ribbon-like pasta** such as *trenette, linguine, bavette...*

• **Long, wide pasta**: *lasagne, pappardelle, reginette*

• **'Nests' or 'coils' of pasta**: *capelli d'angelo, fettuccine, tagliolini, tagliatelle...*

• **Medium-short pasta**: *penne, conchiglie, ruote...*

• **Short, broad pasta:** *maccheroni, sedanini, fusilli...*

Rules
FOR A GOOD PLATE OF PASTA

◆

• The format of the pasta is chosen according to the sauce you wish to make: the bigger the pasta, the richer the sauce. Whereas *capelli d'angelo* can be flavoured with oil (or butter) and cheese, *zite* are better served with meat sauce, cream, mushrooms, etc. while short wide pasta is ideal for oven-baked dishes.

• The pasta should be cooked in plenty of water (around 1 litre for each 100 g). If you are cooking less than half a kilo of pasta the pasta/water ratio changes and you should calculate up to 4 litres of water for every 100 g. The water is brought to the boil in a wide, shallow pot so that the heat is evenly distributed. The liquid should never reach the brim of the pot because the pasta can increase while cooking to three times its dry volume.

• Salt should be added only when the water has begun to boil, calculating about 10 g salt for every litre of water. Salted water in fact boils at a lower temperature than fresh water.

• The pasta is added to the pot, a little at a time, when the water is already boiling. As soon as the water begins to boil again, lower the heat to a simmer. An exception to this rule is filled pasta which is added to the pot a minute before boiling so that the movement of the water does not cause it to break.

• The pasta should be stirred regularly so that it cooks evenly and does not stick. A useful hint, especially for egg or filled pasta, is to add a little oil to the water before adding the pasta.

• The pasta is drained when *al dente* because the less water it absorbs, the more digestible and tastier it will be. If the pasta is to be tossed in the pan or cooked *au gratin* in the oven, it is advisable to drain it slightly before it is completely cooked.
For the cooking time, apart from the indications given on the packet, you can trust in the old 'taste test' (if there is a little white dot in the middle of the spaghetti, it needs to be cooked for 1 minute more).

• Having turned off the heat, halt the cooking process by adding a glass of cold water to the pot, then drain the pasta in a sieve. If you are cooking *gnocchi* or another delicate pasta, drain with the help of a slotted spoon or a large fork, transfer to a deep plate, tip up and let the excess water drain out with the help of a lid.
If the pasta is to be tossed in the sauce or if stipulated in the recipe, leave the pasta in a little cooking water so that it can be mixed better with the sauce.

• For stirring the pasta, cooking the sauce and mixing the ingredients together, always use wooden utensils to avoid the risk of toxic substances or unpleasant flavours contaminating the food and also to avoid breaking the pasta.

- According to tradition, the sequence for flavouring the pasta should be as follows: drain the pasta, transfer it to a serving bowl in which there is some grated cheese (if desired), and then fold in the sauce, mixing gently and carefully to mix in the ingredients.

CARE WITH
OTHER INGREDIENTS

Some final words of advice before you begin to cook. All the ingredients, not only the principal ones, should preferably be **fresh** and of the **best quality**. If you have the opportunity, use products (also meat, eggs, butter etc.) which are grown or raised by natural methods, i.e. without the use of chemical substances or procedures. Make sure that fish, in particular, is fresh, and caught in clean waters.

Nature offers to the cook an inexhaustible source of flavours in the form of **aromatic herbs.** Garlic, basil, bay leaves, fennel, mint, marjoram, chilli peppers etc. often constitute a small but very important ingredient which gives personality to your dish of pasta. Get to know them well so as to use them in the best way in your recipes. Our advice is not to mix too many aromatic herbs together in the one dish and to use them always in moderation in order not to overwhelm the flavour of the other ingredients.

Remember also that the salt most commonly used is produced with dubious refinement processes and is composed almost exclusively of sodium chloride. Refinement processes deprive it of the vital elements which it originally contained and which, even if used as a small percentage, can have an important biological effect. The salt we refer to in the following recipes is not, therefore, refined salt but **sea-salt** which can now be obtained quite easily both in a coarse and a fine form. This salt is not submitted to refinement processes and is rich in elements such as chlorine, sodium, magnesium, sulphur, calcium, potassium, bromine, carbon, strontium, silicon, fluoride, zinc, phosphorous, etc.

CONVERSION CHART

WEIGHT AND LENGTH	SYMBOL	CORRESPONDES TO	SYMBOL	
1 gram (grammo)	g	0.035 ounces	oz	(divide by 28 to find ounces)
1 hectogram (etto)	hg	3.57 ounces	oz	(divide by 0.28 to find ounces)
1 kilogram (chilogrammo)	kg	2.2 pounds	lb	(divide by 0.45 to find pounds)
1 millilitre (millilitro)	ml	0.03 fluid ounces	fl oz	(divide by 30 to find fluid ounces)
1 litre (litro)	l	2.1 pints	pt	(multiply by 2.1 to find pints)
		3.8 gallons (U.S.)	gal	(divide by 0.26 to find U.S. gallons)
		0.22 gallons (U.K.)	gal	(divide by 4.5 to find U.K. gallons)
1 centimeter (centimetro)	cm	0.4 inches	in	(multiply by 0.4 to find inches)
1 millimeter (millimetro)	mm	0.04 inches	in	(multiply by 0.04 to find inches)
1 meter (metro)	m	3.3 feet	ft	(multiply by 3.3 to find feet)

TEMPERATURE

Celsius degree (°C)	(°C x 1.8) + 32 to find Farenheit degree (°F)	180 °C correspondes to 356 °F
Farenheit degree (°F)	(°F – 32) x 555 to find Celsius degree (°C)	392 °F correspondes to 200 °C

NOTE

The quantities in the recipes in the following pages are for 4-6 servings.

PASTA
WITH MEAT

BIGOLI WITH DUCK

◆

400 g bigoli (recipe on page 137), 1 small duck, 1 carrot, 1 onion, 1 stick of celery, 2 garlic cloves, 1 bunch aromatic herbs (bay leaf, rosemary, parsley, basil), 300 g tomato purée, about twenty black olives (optional), halved, with stones removed, 1/4 litre of dry white wine, extra-virgin olive oil, salt, pepper.

Clean the duck and singe it, then lightly brown together with a mixture of chopped carrot, celery, garlic, the herbs and several dessertspoons of olive oil. Add the wine and allow it to evaporate, then add the tomato purée and season with salt and pepper.
Continue cooking for around 2 hours in a covered pot over a moderate heat. If necessary, add a little hot stock or water from time to time.
When the duck is cooked, take it out of the pot, remove the bones and slice the meat. Pass the cooking liquid through a food mill and add the halved olives.
Continue cooking the sauce for around 15 minutes then replace the meat, heat through and use the sauce to flavour the bigoli, which have been cooked in boiling salted water and drained when al dente.

BUCATINI ALL'AMATRICIANA

400 g bucatini, 200 g streaky bacon, 300 g ripe, firm tomatoes, 1/2 onion, stock, extra-virgin olive oil, grated pecorino, salt, chilli powder.

Plunge the tomatoes into hot water, skin them, remove the seeds and chop. Chop the bacon and brown it in several spoonfuls of oil. As soon as the fat has melted, remove from the pan and lay aside. Sauté the sliced onion in the same oil. Add the tomatoes and salt and allow the sauce to thicken for about ten minutes. Replace the cooked bacon and flavour with chilli powder.
Use the sauce to flavour the bucatini, cooked in boiling salted water and drained when al dente. Sprinkle generously with grated pecorino.
The original recipe used little or no tomato and it is thus possible to do without.

BUCATINI WITH LAMB
AND PEPPERS

◆

400 g bucatini, 200 g lamb, 500 g tomato pulp, 2 red or yellow peppers, 2 cloves of garlic, 1 bay leaf, 1/2 glass dry white wine, extra-virgin olive oil, salt, chilli powder.

In an earthenware pot, protected by a heat diffusing plate, flavour several dessertspoons of oil with crushed garlic and a bay leaf, then add the diced lamb and allow to brown.
Remove the garlic cloves and add the wine, allowing it to evaporate over a rapid heat. Clean the peppers, remove seeds and inner filaments, finely chop and add to the lamb. Cook for a few minutes, then add the tomato pulp. Bring sauce to the boil over a rapid heat, lower the heat, cover and continue cooking until the meat is done. Before turning off the heat, check the seasoning and flavour with chilli powder. Cook the bucatini in plentiful salted water, drain when al dente, and drizzle with oil. Transfer to a serving dish and flavour with the sauce.

BUCATINI MARCHIGIANI

◆

400 g bucatini, 100 g mixed Parma ham and bacon, 400 g tomato pulp, 1 onion, 1 carrot, 1 stick celery, red wine, grated pecorino, extra-virgin olive oil, salt, pepper.

Chop together the onion, carrot and celery and sauté in a little oil in a pan. Add the sliced Parma ham and bacon, moisten with wine and allow to evaporate. Add the tomato, a little salt and pepper and cook for around 30 minutes. In the meantime, cook the bucatini, drain when *al dente*, transfer to a warmed soup tureen or serving dish and flavour with the sauce and a generous sprinkling of grated pecorino. Serve piping hot.

CAVATIEDDI WITH HAM

◆

400 g cavatieddi (recipe on page 133), 100 g Parma ham in one slice, 500 g ripe, firm tomatoes, 1 onion, 1 carrot, 1/2 stick celery, red wine, extra-virgin oil, grated pecorino, salt, chilli pepper.

Chop together the onion, carrot and celery and sauté in oil in an earthenware pot. Add the ham which has been chopped into little squares, cook for a little and then add the wine. Continue cooking until the wine evaporates. Skin the tomatoes after plunging them into hot water, remove the seeds, chop and add to the mixture. Add salt and a pinch of chilli powder, and allow to cook for around 20 minutes.
Cook the cavatieddi in plentiful salted water, drain when *al dente* and flavour with the sauce and a generous sprinkling of grated pecorino.

FARFALLE WITH TURKEY AND PEA SAUCE

◆

400 g farfalle (butterfly-shaped pasta), 200 g turkey breast, 100 g bacon, 500 g ripe, firm tomatoes, 200 g fresh shelled peas, 1 onion, marjoram, extra-virgin olive oil, salt, pepper.

Chop the onion and sauté in several spoonfuls of oil together with the chopped bacon. Add the turkey meat, cut into thin slices, and allow the flavours to blend.
Plunge the tomatoes into boiling water, skin, remove the seeds, chop and cook together with the peas which have been softened in boiling salted water for about ten minutes. Allow the sauce to thicken and season with salt, pepper and marjoram. Continue cooking, adding a few drops of water from time to time if the sauce becomes too dry. Cook the farfalle in boiling salted water, drain when *al dente* and mix with the sauce.

FETTUCCINE ALLA PAPALINA

◆

400 g fettuccine (recipe on page 138), 100 g Parma ham in thin slices, 200 g small peas, 1/2 onion, 2 eggs, 4 dessertspoons of grated parmesan, extra-virgin olive oil, salt, freshly ground pepper.

Sauté the chopped onion in a few spoonfuls of oil over a rapid heat, add the peas and season with salt and pepper. Lower the heat, cover and continue to cook, adding a little hot water from time to time if necessary. Just before turning off the heat, cut the ham into thin slices and add to the peas. In the meantime, in a warmed serving bowl, beat the eggs with the parmesan, a pinch of salt and some freshly ground pepper. Cook the pasta and when *al dente*, drain, transfer to the soup tureen and add the pea sauce. Mix well before serving.

FETTUCCINE
ALLLA ROMANA

◆

400 g fettuccine (recipe on page 138), 300 g beef, 500 g ripe, firm, tomatoes, 1 onion, 1 carrot, 1 stick celery, 1/2 glass red wine, 1 dessertspoon lard, salt, chilli powder.

Sauté the chopped onion, carrots and celery in the lard, add the beef cut into little pieces and sprinkle with chilli powder.
Add some wine and allow to evaporate. Skin the tomatoes, remove the seeds, chop and add to the beef sauce. Check salt and continue cooking. Boil the fettuccine in salted water, drain when al dente, transfer to a serving dish and serve piping hot, flavoured with the meat sauce.

FILATIEDDI
WITH SAUCE

◆

400 g filatieddi (recipe on page 137), 800 g shoulder of lamb, 500 g ripe, firm tomatoes, 80 g dried mushrooms, 1/2 onion, 1 dessertspoon chopped parsley, 1 pinch chilli powder, 60 g grated pecorino, 1 dessertspoon flour, 1/2 glass dry white wine, 10 g lard, 2 dessertspoons extra-virgin olive oil, salt.

Melt the lard in a saucepan, add the diced lamb, season with salt and chilli powder and cook, covered, over a low heat for 25 minutes.
In the meantime, soften the dried mushrooms in lukewarm water for about 15 minutes, drain and slice. Remove the lamb from the pot and keep warm: add the oil and mushrooms to the cooking juices in the pot, cook over a moderate heat for a few minutes.
Remove the mushrooms and mix with the lamb. Add the finely chopped onion to the cooking juices and cook till it becomes transparent. Add the wine and allow to evaporate.
Remove from heat, add the flour, then replace on the heat; as soon as the flour begins to brown add the tomatoes which have been passed through a food mill, adjust seasoning to taste and continue to cook for 20 minutes. Replace the lamb and mushrooms, cover the pot and cook for a further 10 minutes. Finally add the chopped parsley.
In the meantime, bring to the boil a pot of salted water. Boil the filatieddi, drain when *al dente*, transfer to a serving dish, blend well into the sauce and add a generous sprinkling of grated pecorino.

FUSILLI
WITH SAUSAGE
AND PORCINI MUSHROOMS

◆

400 g fusilli (short, curly pasta), 200 g sausage, 300 g fresh porcini mushrooms or 30 g dried mushrooms, 300 g tomato pulp, 1 onion, 1 small carrot, 1 bay leaf, marjoram, extra-virgin olive oil, salt, pepper.

Clean the mushrooms carefully and dice. If you are using dried mushrooms, steep them first in lukewarm water. Chop the onion and carrot and sauté in a few spoonfuls of oil in a pot. When the onion is transparent, add the skinned and sliced sausage, the mushrooms and a crushed bayleaf.

Stirring carefully, allow to cook for a few minutes, then add the tomato pulp, salt and pepper; lower the heat, cover the pot and continue cooking until the sauce has thickened. If necessary, from time to time add some hot water or stock (or alternatively use the liquid in which the mushrooms have been steeping, filtered through a cotton cloth). Before removing from the heat flavour the sauce with finely chopped marjoram.

A different flavour may be obtained by combining sausages with artichokes: remove the points and the outer leaves from the latter, cut into wedges and steep in water and lemon

juice. before adding to the mixture of onion and carrot in the pot.

In both cases the sauce used to flavour the cooked fusilli should be very hot.

GARGANELLI
ALLA BOSCAIOLA

◆

400 g garganelli (recipe on page 137), 200 g porcini mushrooms, 150 g thick-cut bacon, 4 tomatoes for sauce, 1 clove garlic, 30 g butter, 1 sprig of parsley, Parmesan cheese, salt, pepper.

Clean the mushrooms with a little brush and a cotton rag without using water, slice finely and sauté with the chopped bacon and the crushed garlic in butter, over a moderate heat, while stirring with a wooden spoon.

Plunge the tomatoes into hot water, skin them, remove the seeds, chop and add to the mushroom and bacon. Allow to cook over a low heat until the

24

sauce has thickened; remove the garlic. Cook the garganelli in plentiful salted water, drain when *al dente*, transfer to a large dish. Add the sauce, garnish with chopped parsley and sprinkle generously with grated Parmesan. Serve immediately.

GARGANELLI SAPORITI

◆

400 g garganelli (recipe on page 137), 100 g minced meat, 1 cup tomato sauce, 1 cup bechamel sauce, 1 leek, 1 sprig rosemary, extra-virgin oil, Parmesan cheese, salt, pepper.

In oil flavoured with the rosemary, sauté the finely chopped leek until it is transparent Add the minced meat, a pinch each of salt and pepper and allow to brown. Add the tomato sauce and cook until the sauce has thickened. Cook the garganelli in salted water, drain and transfer to the pot with the sauce. Add the béchamel and mix together. Remove from the heat, sprinkle with Parmesan cheese and serve piping hot.

MACCHERONI
WITH MEAT BALLS

◆

400 g maccheroni, 200 g minced beef, 500 g tomato pulp, 1/2 onion, 1 small carrot, 1/2 stick celery, 1 bunch parsley, 1 bay leaf, 1 clove garlic, basil, 2 dessertspoons grated Parmesan, breadcrumbs of 1 stale roll, 1 egg, milk, extra-virgin oil, salt, chilli powder.

Soften the breadcrumbs in a little milk, squeeze out the moisture and add to the minced beef with a little parsley,

crushed garlic, a sprinkling of grated cheese, a pinch of salt and one of chilli powder. Mix all the ingredients together carefully, binding with the yolk of an egg, The mixture should not be too soft or the meatballs will crumble in the sauce. Form little balls about the size of a large olive and brown them evenly in the oil; when they have turned golden, drain and keep to one side. Clean the pot and replace over heat with 2-3 dessertspoons of new oil and a mixture of diced onion, celery and carrot.

Sauté the vegetables; when soft, add the tomato pulp, salt and bay leaf and continue to cook. A few minutes before turning off the heat, remove the bay leaf, add the meat balls to the sauce with a little chilli powder and the chopped basil; allow the flavours to blend then remove from the heat.

Boil the maccheroni in salted water and drain when *al dente*, mix with a part of the sauce, spoon over the remaining sauce and a generous sprinkling of grated Parmesan.

MACCHERONI
WITH SAUSAGE AND RICOTTA

◆

400 g maccheroni, 400 g ricotta, 150 g sausage, grated pecorino, extra-virgin olive oil, salt, pepper.

Cream the ricotta in a large bowl with salt, a generous grinding of pepper and the skinned sausage which has been browned in its own fat over a low heat. When the mixture is rich and creamy, put it aside and cook the pasta in plentiful salted water. Drain the maccheroni when *al dente*, but save a few spoonfuls of the cooking water. Transfer the pasta to a serving dish with the ricotta and mix carefully with the salted water, a sprinkling of grated pecorino and a drizzle of oil.

MALLOREDDUS
WITH WILD BOAR SAUCE

◆

400 g malloreddus (recipe on page 133), 450 g minced cinghiale (wild boar), 450 g tomato sauce, 1 onion, some bay leaves, grated pecorino, extra-virgin olive oil, salt, pepper.

Sauté the onion in a generous quantity of oil, add the minced meat, flavour with a pinch of salt and one of pepper, and leave to brown for a few minutes. Add the tomato sauce with some bay leaves, and cook slowly for two hours. After cooking the malloreddus in plentiful salted water, drain and flavour with the sauce and the grated pecorino.

ORECCHIETTE
ALLA LUCANA

◆

400 g orecchiette (recipe on page 135), 300 g minced veal, 500 g ripe, firm tomatoes, 1 onion, a few basil leaves, extra virgin oil, grated pecorino, salt, chilli powder.

Finely chop the onion and soften in a few spoonfuls of oil in an earthenware pot; as soon as it is transparent add the minced meat and salt, stir and allow to cook for a few minutes. Plunge the tomatoes into boiling water, remove the skins and seeds, then cook over a low heat for around 2 hours, stirring from time to time. If necessary, add some hot water. Before turning off the heat check the seasoning and add a little chilli powder and the crushed basil.

Boil the orecchiette in plentiful salted water, drain and flavour with the sauce and a sprinkling of grated pecorino.

PAPPARDELLE
WITH VENISON
AND PORCINI MUSHROOMS

400 g pappardelle (recipe on page 138), 350 g leg of venison, 150 g porcini mushrooms, 1/2 litre red wine, 1 small onion, 1 small carrot, 2 bay leaves, 1 small sprig rosemary, 40 g butter, Parmesan cheese, salt, pepper.

Cut the meat into cubes and marinate for 12 hours in the red wine, (keeping a glassful aside) with the aromatic herbs and the peeled and roughly chopped carrot and onion. At the end of this time remove the meat, herbs and vegetables. Mix together the herbs and vegetables and sauté in a little butter.

Clean the mushrooms with a little brush and a cotton rag and slice finely. Sauté separately in a little butter. Add the meat cubes and allow to brown over a moderate heat for a few minutes. Moisten with the glass of red wine, add salt and pepper; lower the flame, cover the pot and cook for 30 minutes.

At the end of this time add the cooked vegetables to the meat and mushrooms. Boil the pasta in salted water,

drain when al dente and transfer to the pan containing the sauce. Sauté together for a couple of minutes and serve with a generous sprinkling of grated Parmesan.

PAPPARDELLE
WITH WILD BOAR

◆

400 g pappardelle (recipe on page 138), 400 g roughly minced lean wild boar meat, 350 g tomato pulp, 1 dessertspoon tomato concentrate, 1 onion, 1 small carrot, 1 celery stick, 2 bay leaves, 1 glass of red wine, extra-virgin olive oil, salt, chilli powder.

In a little oil sauté a mixture of finely chopped onion, carrot and celery, add the minced meat and allow to brown. Add the red wine and allow to evaporate. Add the tomato pulp and the tomato concentrate diluted in a little hot water. Add salt, chilli powder and the bay leaves and cook over a low heat for around an hour and a half.

Boil the pappardelle in salted water, drain when al dente and toss in the meat sauce before serving.
A variation to this recipe suggests using 2 parts boar meat and 1 part beef to reduce the gamy flavour which is typical of wild boar. It is also possible to use only tomato concentrate and to do without the tomato pulp.

PAPPARDELLE
WITH HARE SAUCE

400 g pappardelle (recipe on page 138), 1 small hare, 50 g bacon, 1/2 onion, 1 small carrot, 1/2 stick celery, 1 clove garlic, rosemary, 1 dessertspoon tomato concentrate,(or 1.5 dl. milk), 1 glass red wine, extra-virgin olive oil, salt, pepper.

Clean the hare, keeping the front part (head and shoulders) and the heart and liver for the sauce; wash under cold running water, dry and cut into pieces, taking care not to break the bones. In a few spoonfuls of oil sauté a mixture of chopped bacon, garlic, onion, carrots and celery; as soon as the vegetables begin to soften, add the pieces of hare including the entrails. Allow to brown over a moderate heat, add the wine, allow to evaporate and season with salt, pepper and rosemary. After a few minutes add the tomato concentrate diluted in a little hot water; lower the heat, cover the pot and continue cooking for about half an hour. If necessary, add a little stock or hot water from time to time.
Towards the end of the cooking time, take the hare pieces out of the pot and remove the bones; pass the sauce through a sieve, then return to the heat, with the chopped meat and entrails. Heat the sauce well before mixing in the pasta which has been cooked in boiling salted water and drained when al dente.

A version of this recipe suggests the use of milk rather than tomato.

PAPPARDELLE
WITH PHEASANT

◆

400 g pappardelle (recipe on page 138), 1/2 pheasant, 1 small glass of cognac, 1 glass dry white wine, 1 cup vegetable stock, a few sage leaves, 1 sprig rosemary, 60 g butter, 1 dessertspoon cream, Parmesan cheese, salt.

Pluck and bone the pheasant, clean and wash it under running cold water, dry and slice into small strips. Sauté in 30 g butter with some bay leaves. When the meat is golden brown, add the cognac, white wine and allow to evaporate. Lower the heat, cover the pot and continue to cook for half an hour, moistening from time to time with the hot vegetable stock. Pass the pheasant liver and the cooking liquid through a sieve. In a separate pot melt some butter and flavour with the rosemary. Cook the pasta in plentiful salted water, drain when al dente, transfer to the pot with the pheasant meat. Add the liver cooking juices, the melted rosemary butter and the cream and mix together. Sprinkle generously with grated Parmesan.

PENNE CUBAN STYLE

◆

400 g penne, 100 g cooked ham in one slice, 300 g fresh mushrooms, 300 g ripe, firm tomatoes (optional), 1 clove garlic, 1 small bunch parsley, 1/4 litre cream, extra-virgin olive oil, salt, chilli powder.

Clean the mushrooms carefully without using water but removing any grit with a cotton rag, and slice. Heat a few dessertspoons of oil in a pan and flavour with crushed garlic. As soon as the garlic begins to brown, remove it and add the mushrooms to the oil. If using tomatoes, remove the skins by first plunging them into hot water, remove the seeds and chop. Add the tomatoes to the oil, cover the pot and continue cooking over a moderate heat. If necessary, add a little salted water or hot stock. In a bowl, mix the ham cut into cubes, the cream, a little chilli powder and some finely chopped parsley.
Boil the pasta, drain when al dente and transfer to the pan with the mushroom sauce. Add the cream and ham and mix carefully. Serve piping hot.

PICI
WITH RABBIT SAUCE

◆

400 g pici (recipe on page 135), 1/2 rabbit, 300 g tomato sauce, 100 g bacon, 1 onion, 1 carrot, 2 celery sticks, 2 cloves garlic, 2 bay leaves, 1/2 litre red wine, extra-virgin olive oil, salt, pepper.

In a large dish marinate the rabbit overnight in wine with the aromatic herbs and the roughly chopped vegetables.

Next day, remove the vegetables, chop them finely and sauté in a little oil with some chopped bacon. Remove the rabbit from the marinade, cut it into pieces and add to the sauté mixture. Allow the rabbit to absorb the flavours, then moisten with wine from the marinade and wait till it evaporates almost completely. Add the tomato sauce, adjust the seasoning, cover the pot and continue cooking over a moderate heat for about an hour and a half. When the sauce is ready remove the rabbit, bone and cut it into pieces. Blend the cooking juices to a creamy sauce, replace the pieces of meat. Allow to rest while you prepare the pasta. Boil the pici in salted water and drain when *al dente*. Return the sauce to the heat, add the pasta and toss together for a minute.

PISAREI, PORK SAUSAGE AND PEPPERS

◆

400 g pisarei (recipe on page 136), 1/2 cotechino (pork sausage), 1 pepper, 1 clove garlic, 1 ladle tomato conserve, extra-virgin olive oil, grated Parmesan, salt.

Boil the pork sausage (if you are using a packaged traditional cotechino, follow the instructions on the packet; if you use home-made cotechino, keep it wrapped in a white cloth, sewn at the ends, while cooking). Skin the sausage and cut it into tiny cubes. Scorch the pepper on all sides in the oven, remove the burnt skin and

the seeds and inner filaments. Cut into small slices. Sauté the pork sausage cubes in the oil with the pepper strips, garlic and a little salt. Add the tomato conserve and allow to cook for a few minutes. Cook the pasta, drain when *al dente* and transfer to the pot with the sauce. Sauté for a couple of minutes, sprinkle with grated Parmesan and serve hot.

PIZZOCCHERI WITH COOKED HAM

◆

400 g pizzoccheri (recipe on page 136), 150 g thickly sliced cooked ham, 40 g butter, 2 dessertspoons single cream, 2 sage leaves, grated Parmesan, nutmeg, salt.

Cut the ham into match-stick slices. Melt a little butter in a pan and add the sage leaves. Cook the pizzoccheri in salted water, drain and transfer to the pan; add the melted butter, the ham, the cream, the salt and some grated nutmeg. Mix all together and toss over a moderate heat for two or three minutes. Serve immediately, sprinkled generously with grated Parmesan.

31

REGINETTE
WITH SPECK

◆

400 g reginette, 200 g thickly sliced speck, 100 g fresh peas (shelled), 2 cloves garlic, 1/2 glass dry white wine, extra-virgin olive oil, grated Parmesan, salt, pepper.

Blanch the peas in boiling salted water for about ten minutes; drain. Cut the speck into cubes and sauté in a few spoonfuls of oil with the sliced garlic cloves and the peas. As soon as the garlic begins to colour, remove from the pan. Add wine to the peas and allow to evaporate; add salt, pepper and continue cooking over a moderate heat for about ten minutes. In the meantime cook the reginette in plentiful salted water, drain when al dente and transfer to the pot with the speck and peas. Mix together over the heat for a few minutes and season with a grinding of pepper, and a sprinkling of grated cheese.
To vary this recipe you can add 2-3 dessertspoons of cream to the speck to bind the mixture together.

32

REGINETTE
WITH SNAIL SAUCE

◆

400 g reginette, 1 kg snails, 500 g firm, ripe tomatoes, 1 onion, 1 celery stick, 1 clove garlic, 1 bay leaf, 1 bunch aromatic herbs (rosemary, thyme, basil), 1 sprig parsley, 1 glass white wine, maize meal, grated Parmesan, extra-virgin olive oil, salt, pepper.

Clean the snails and prepare them for cooking: boil them for ten minutes in salted water with some aromatic herbs. Plunge them into cold water to cool, drain, remove the shells and clean away the entrails. Transfer the snails to a bowl containing the maize meal and rub them with your hands in the flour to get rid of any residual liquids. Wash again and dry. They are now ready for cooking.
In a pot (preferably earthenware), sauté the chopped onion, crushed garlic and bay leaf, add the snails, mix together and add the finely chopped celery and parsley.
Cover the pot and allow the flavours to blend for several minutes over a low heat. Moisten with the wine, raise the heat and allow the wine to evaporate. Add the tomatoes (previously skinned and chopped with seeds removed). Lower the heat and allow the sauce to thicken. Finally add salt, pepper and a handful of finely chopped aromatic herbs.
Cook the reginette in salted water, drain when al dente; serve in a warmed tureen, with the snail sauce and sprinkled generously with grated Parmesan.

SPAGHETTI
ALLA CHITARRA
WITH RAGU SAUCE

◆

400 g spaghetti (recipe on page 136), 500 g pork in one slice, 4 slices of bacon, 1 piece of bacon fat, 500 g firm, ripe tomatoes, 3 garlic cloves, a small bunch parsley, red wine, 1 dessertspoon lard, fresh pecorino, salt, pepper.

Chop 2 cloves of garlic with a little parsley and make a paste with the chopped bacon fat and a little freshly ground pepper. Spread over the slice of pork, beaten out thin with a meat pound or the blade of a knife. Place the bacon slices over the paste and top with a few pieces of pecorino. Roll up the meat and close with a toothpick or cooking thread.

Cut the remaining lard into pieces and melt in an earthenware pot along with the remaining garlic clove. Brown the meat, add a little wine and as soon as it has evaporated, add some salt and pepper. Remove the skins and seeds from the tomatoes, chop and add to the meat. Continue to cook the sauce; a minute before turning off the heat, remove the meat and keep aside.

Boil the spaghetti in salted water, drain when *al dente* and flavour with the sauce: cut the meat into slices and serve as a second course.

TAGLIATELLE
WITH RABBIT SAUCE

◆

400 g tagliatelle (recipe on page 138), 200 g rabbit meat, 1 clove garlic, a few sprigs of rosemary, 1 dessertspoon white flour, 1/2 glass dry white wine, extra-virgin oil, butter, salt, pepper.

Cut the rabbit meat into small pieces and marinate in wine, a little salt and pepper and add the shredded rosemary. Drain after an hour and brown in a few spoonfuls of oil which has been previously flavoured with the garlic clove. When the meat is a nice golden colour, add the salt and continue cooking, moistening now and then with some of the marinade.

Remove the rabbit from the sauce and keep to one side; add a knob of butter to the cooking juices and mix in the flour.

33

As soon as the sauce thickens, replace the rabbit, stir in the pasta which has been cooked to *al dente* and drained.

TAGLIATELLE
WITH BOLOGNESE SAUCE

◆

400 g tagliatelle (recipe on page 138), 200 g minced beef, 50 g bacon, 1/2 onion, 1 small carrot, 1/2 stick celery, 2 dessertspoons tomato concentrate, 1/2 glass red wine, stock, extra-virgin olive oil, salt, pepper.

Finely slice the onion, carrot and celery and, separately, the bacon. Brown the latter in a few spoonfuls of oil (not too much oil if the bacon is fatty). When the fat has melted, add the chopped vegetables, stirring carefully. As soon as the mixture has softened add the meat. Keep stirring so that the meat turns an even brown colour. Add the wine and allow to evaporate.

Add the tomato concentrate diluted with a little hot stock and salt and pepper. Lower the heat and continue cooking with the lid on for around 2 hours. Moisten from time to time with a little hot stock.

Boil the tagliatelle, drain when *al dente*, mix with some of the meat sauce. Serve with the remaining sauce in a sauce boat, and grated parmesan on the side.

There are several variations: you can also use mixed minced meats, add some chopped chicken liver, flavour with dry mushrooms and the water used for steeping, do without the tomato etc.

SPAGHETTI
ALLA CARBONARA

400 g spaghetti, 200 g bacon, 1 clove garlic, 3 dessertspoons of grated Parmesan, 3 spoonfuls of grated pecorino, 2 eggs and 2 egg yolks, extra-virgin olive oil, salt, pepper.

Dice the bacon into 5 mm cubes and brown in a pan with a few spoonfuls of oil and the garlic clove (which you should remove as soon as it begins to colour).

In a warmed serving bowl, blend 2 whole eggs and 2 yolks at room temperature with the grated cheeses. Season with a pinch of salt and plenty of freshly ground pepper, and thoroughly until you have a smooth, creamy sauce.

The sauce should be prepared when the pasta is just about ready. Drain the pasta, transfer it to the serving bowl, mix with the egg and the crunchy hot bacon and serve piping hot.

TAGLIOLINI
WITH CHICKEN LIVER SAUCE

◆

400 g tagliolini (recipe on page 138), 300 g chicken heart and livers, 1/2 onion, 2 sage leaves, 1 dessertspoon tomato concentrate or 3 dessertspoons cream, dry white wine, butter, salt.

Finely chop the onion and soften in a pot with a knob of butter and the sage leaves; add the roughly chopped chicken hearts and allow to brown. Remove the sage, add the wine and allow to evaporate. If desired, add the tomato concentrate, diluted in a little hot water. Just before the hearts are cooked add the chicken livers which have been cleaned and roughly chopped, add salt, and allow the flavours to blend. If you prefer not to use the tomato, blend the cream into the sauce a minute before turning off the heat. Cook the tagliolini in plentiful salted water and drain when al dente, then fold carefully into the sauce and serve.

VERMICELLI
WITH CHICKEN
AND TRUFFLE

◆

400 g vermicelli, 1 medium-sized white truffle, 1 chicken breast, tongue, 1 mozzarella, 150 g new peas, 1 tomato, 1/2 glass meat roasting juices, grated Parmesan, buttor or extra-virgin olive oil, salt.

This is a recipe with a variety of ingredients which offers great scope to the imagination and taste of each individual cook.
Cook the vermicelli in salted water and drain them when they are al dente. Flavour with butter (or oil), grated Parmesan and the roasting juices. Transfer to an ovenproof dish, shape the pasta into a mound and then decorate with strips of chicken breast and tongue which have been cooked separately, with the fresh peas cooked in butter, and with slices of tomato topping the whole off with thin slices of truffle. Mix in a little more of the roasting juices and sprinkle with grated Parmesan. Cut the mozzarella into slices and then fan them out over the pasta.
Place the dish in a hot oven until the mozzarella begins to melt. Remove from the oven and serve.

PASTA
WITH FISH

BAVETTE
WITH FISH

◆

400 g bavette, 600 g mixed seafood such as baby squid, small cuttlefish, scampi and shrimp, 3 cloves of garlic, a small bunch parsley, 1/2 glass of white wine, extra-virgin olive oil, salt, chilli powder

Remove any small bones or fins from the seafood as well as eyes, beaks or entrails (which are extracted by pulling the tentacles, taking care not to break the ink sac which can be used to flavour this or another sauce). Wash them and if the bodies are large, cut them into little strips, leaving the little tentacles intact. Shellfish need not be shelled; just washed carefully. Cut the shrimps into cubes since the flesh can be 'sucked' out.

In a large pot, heat a few dessertspoons of oil with the crushed garlic and the chilli powder; add the fish and when it has been heated on all sides, add the wine and allow it to evaporate.

The traditional recipe then suggests that the bavette be broken and added to the pot with the fish along with some boiling water, and cooked like risotto.

If you don't feel up to this recipe, boil the pasta in the normal way, drain when al dente and mix in with the sauce before serving.

In both cases, just before turning off the heat stir in a generous sprinkling of chopped parsley.

BIGOLI
WITH SARDINES

◆

400 g bigoli (recipe on page 137), 6 sardines, 1 clove garlic, a small bunch parsley, 1 glass of extra-virgin olive oil, salt.

This is a typical dish from the region of Veneto, and the sardines used in the traditional recipe were those fished in Lake Garda itself.

You can, however, use tinned sardines which should be cleaned (without using water, if possible), boned, and then treated in the same way.

Clean the sardines, removing the heads, bones and tails; wash them and leave to dry on a tea-cloth and then cut into little pieces. Cook in hot oil until they begin to disintegrate and just before turning off the heat, add a mixture of chopped garlic and parsley. Cook the bigoli in salted water, drain while they are still al dente and blend thoroughly into the sauce.

38

BUCATINI
WITH SQUID

◆

400 g bucatini, 4-5 squid (about. 500 g), 500 g spinach, 500 g firm, ripe tomatoes, 200 g mushrooms, 1 clove garlic, 1 small bunch parsley, 1 egg, 2 dessertspoons grated Parmesan. 1-2 dessertspoons breadcrumbs, extra-virgin olive oil, salt, chilli powder.

Clean the vegetables, using a cotton rag to clean the grit and earth from the mushrooms. Boil the spinach in salted water, drain and squeeze out the excess water. Slice the mushrooms and sauté in a few dessertspoons of oil, salt and pepper. Mix with the cooked spinach.

Clean the squid; separate the tentacles from the body (discarding the entrails and taking care not to break the ink sacs). Chop the tentacles and mix with the vegetables together with a little chopped parsley, egg, cheese, breadcrumbs, a pinch of salt and one of pepper. Mix carefully to obtain a smooth mixture which is then used to stuff the squid. Sew with kitchen thread.

Skin the tomatoes by plunging them in hot water, remove the seeds and chop. Heat a few spoonfuls of oil and flavour with a crushed garlic clove; as soon as the garlic begins to colour, remove it and add the tomatoes.

When the sauce begins to simmer, add the squid, a pinch of salt and one of chilli powder; cover and cook for about 30-40 minutes, then drain the fish and keep it warm together with a few spoonfuls of the sauce.

Boil the bucatini in salted water and drain when al dente. Mix into the sauce in the pot, sprinkle with chopped parsley and drizzle with oil.

Garnish with the sliced, stuffed squid and the remaining sauce.

BUCATINI
WITH FRIED FISH

◆

400 g bucatini, 400 g small frying fish, 1 ripe but firm tomato, 3 garlic cloves, 1 small bunch parsley, 1 handful basil leaves, handful celery leaves, white flour, extra-virgin olive oil, salt, pepper.

Plunge the tomato in boiling water so it can be skinned easily, remove the seeds, cut into wedges, sprinkle with salt and leave for a while to drain. Chop roughly and mix in a large bowl with the peeled garlic cloves, cut in half, and leave to rest for about 30 minutes. Remove the garlic, drizzle with oil, season with salt and pepper and sprinkle with finely chopped herbs. Wash and dry the fish carefully, roll in the flour and fry in hot oil.

39

In the meantime cook the bucatini in salted water, drain, mix with the seasoned tomato and garnish with the fried fish.

Boil the bucatini and when *al dente*, drain and stir into the sauce and serve garnished with the whole sardines and a sprinkling of fresh chopped parsley.

BUCATINI
WITH SARDINES
AND FENNEL

◆

400 g bucatini, 800 g sardines, 150 g fennel hearts, 2 cloves garlic, 1 dessertspoon raisins, 1 dessertspoon pine-nuts, 1 sprig parsley, breadcrumbs, extra-virgin olive oil, salt, chilli powder.

Clean the sardines, rinse and leave to dry on a dish-cloth. Blanch the fennel hearts in boiling salted water for a few minutes, drain and cut into wedges. Steep the raisins in lukewarm water for fifteen minutes. Crush the garlic and sauté in a few spoonfuls of oil. As soon as the garlic begins to brown, remove and add the sardines to the oil: cook on both sides for a few minutes. Add the raisins, (drained), the pine-nuts, a dessertspoon of chopped parsley, a dessertspoon of breadcrumbs, a pinch of salt and one of chilli powder. Cook the sauce over a moderate heat, shaking the pan gently by the handle every now and then so as not to break the sardines. Just before turning off the heat remove the sardines and set aside.

BASKETS
OF SPAGHETTI
AND SEAFOOD

◆

250 g larger-sized spaghetti, 300 g shelled prawns, 16 scallops. 2 cloves garlic, 1 small bunch parsley, 1 glass dry white wine, extra virgin olive oil, salt, pepper.

Scrub the scallops, place them in a large pot with a clove of garlic and half a glass of wine, cover and allow to open over a moderate heat. Turn off the heat, remove the scallops and filter the cooking liquid. Free the fish from the shell, remove the inedible parts, separate the roe from the white flesh and keep the roe aside.

In a large pot heat 3-4 dessertspoons oil with a clove of garlic which should be removed as soon as it starts to turn golden. Add the sliced scallops and sauté for a couple of

minutes over a rapid heat. Add the prawns and sauté for a further two minutes. Add half a glass of wine and allow to evaporate.

Add a little of the cooking juice of the scallops, add plenty of pepper, a little salt and cook for a further 4-5 minutes. The sauce should be allowed to dry almost completely. Add the chopped parsley, cover and keep warm. Cook the spaghetti in salted water, drain when al dente, spread out on the plate and drizzle with oil so it doesn't stick. Divide the spaghetti into eight portions and place the first portion in a wire scoop to form a nest.

Heat up plenty of oil in a deep pot, dip the nest into the oil and allow it to turn golden. Drain well, remove the pasta from the scoop and keep warm. Repeat with the other portions of spaghetti.

Arrange the nests of pasta on a serving dish. Add the roe of the scallop to the seafood mixture, mix and fill each nest with the sauce.

FARFALLE
WITH SCALLOPS
AND ASPARAGUS

◆

350 g farfalle, (butterly-shaped pasta) 150 g asparagus, 150 g shelled scallops, 150 g single cream, 100 g porcini mushrooms, 1 shallot, 1 sprig parsley, 30 g dry vermouth, butter, extra-virgin olive oil, salt, pepper.

Clean the asparagus by scraping the stem and cutting off the tough leathery part at the bottom; rinse and cook in boiling water for a few minutes.

Drain and cut into slices. Clean the mushrooms with a cotton rag, cut into slices, keeping the heads separate from the stems Sauté the stems in three spoonfuls of olive oil over a moderate heat for a minute, then add the heads. Sauté for a few minutes more, add salt, pepper and turn off the heat. Clean and chop the shallot and cook in 20 g butter until transparent. Add the sliced scallops, season with salt and pepper and allow to brown. Add 30 g dry vermouth. When the liquid has evaporated, add the mushrooms and the asparagus. Continue cooking over quite a rapid heat, allow the sauce to reduce a little, then add the cream, lower the flame, adjust seasoning. Cook the farfalle in salted water, drain when al dente, mix with the sauce and serve sprinkled with a spoonful of chopped parsley.

FETTUCCINE
WITH OVEN-BAKED SOLE

◆

400 g fettuccine (recipe on page 133), 4-5 sole fillets, (about 800 g), 150 g mussels, 150 g prawns, 150 g champignon mushrooms, 1/2 lemon, paprika, 2 egg yolks, 1.5 dl. single cream, 1.5 dl. dry white wine, extra-virgin olive oil, 30 g butter, salt, pepper.

Wash and shell the prawns. Clean the mussels and allow them to open over a moderate heat in a covered pan with one or two spoonfuls of oil; as they open separate the mussels from the shell. Clean any grit or earth from the mushrooms with a damp cloth, slice, sauté together with the prawns and the mussels in a few spoonfuls of oil. Add salt and pepper and allow to cook for a few minutes. Remove from the heat.

In an ovenproof dish heat a few spoonfuls of oil and brown the sole on both sides, add the wine and a pinch each of paprika, salt and pepper. Place in a hot oven (180° C) until the fish is cooked.

Remove from the oven, drain the fish and filter the cooking juices. Cook this liquid in a pan over the heat until it is reduced. Stirring all the time, add the cream and a little filtered lemon juice, the egg yolks, the butter cut into pieces and some freshly ground pepper (one turn of the mill). Allow to thicken.

Cook the fettuccine in salted water and drain when *al dente*; drizzle with oil and transfer to a serving dish. Lay the fish fillets over the pasta and add the mushroom and seafood sauce. Mix all together with the cream sauce.

Place in a hot oven and cook au gratin at 200°C. Serve piping hot.

FETTUCCINE
WITH CRAB

◆

400 g fettuccine (recipe on page 133), 4 crabs or 'gnacchere', 1 small onion, 1 clove garlic, 40 g wild fennel, 200 g ripe tomatoes, extra-virgin olive oil, dry white wine, salt.

The original recipe calls for 'gnacchere', molluscs found off the Sardinian coast with a beautiful shell which gives this dish its spectacular appearance. The taste of the gnacchere, however, is almost identical to that of crabmeat, which can be obtained more

easily. Crab can thus be used without altering the taste of this recipe in any way.

Plunge the tomatoes into hot water for a few minutes, remove the skins and seeds and chop into cubes. Finely chop the onion and the garlic. Scoop out the crabmeat, and cut into pieces. Sauté the onion and garlic in the oil, add the wine and allow to evaporate; then add the crab. Cook for a few minutes over a moderate heat, remove from the heat and add the tomatoes. In a little mildly salted water in a pot, boil the fennel for 10 minutes, add the pasta and cook: the liquid should be almost completely dried up. Drain the pasta, mix in the sauce, adjust the salt and add the oil. Mix carefully and serve.

FUSILLI
WITH SCAMPI
AND ZUCCHINI

📷

400 g fusilli, 450 g scampi, 350 g zucchini, 1 shallot, 1 sprig of parsley, 1/2 litre of fish stock, extra-virgin olive oil, salt, pepper.

Cut zucchini into julienne strips and clean the scampi carefully. Sauté the finely chopped shallot in a few spoonfuls of oil and as soon as it becomes transparent, add the zucchini and the scampi. Add salt and pepper and cook over a low heat, adding a little fish stock. Boil the fusilli in plentiful salted water and drain when *al dente*. Mix in the sauce, drizzle with oil and sprinkle with a handful of chopped parsley.

LINGUINE
AND SEAFOOD

◆

400 g linguine, 500 g mussels, 400 g clams, 500 g firm, ripe tomatoes, 3 cloves garlic, a few basil leaves, 2 sprigs oregano, extra-virgin olive oil, salt, chilli powder.

Scrub the shells of the mussels and clams, and steep in salted water for at least half an hour to get rid of any sand. Heat some oil over a rapid heat, add one crushed garlic clove and fresh oregano to taste, add the shellfish and allow to open. As they open, split the shells into two, discarding the empty half. When all have opened, turn off the heat, filter and keep the cooking juices to one side. Skin the tomatoes by plunging them into hot water, remove the seeds and chop roughly. Heat a few spoonfuls of oil with the two remaining garlic cloves; add the tomatoes and allow them to dry for a few minutes over a rapid heat, then lower the heat, add salt and a little chilli powder.

Boil the linguine in plentiful salted water, drain when *al dente*. Mix in the sauce and add the half mussels and clams, a mixture of chopped basil and oregano and a ladle of filtered juices from the shellfish.

Mix carefully, then transfer the pasta and sauce to a sheet of silver foil, cover and pinch the edges together (don't allow the foil to stick to the food). Place in a very hot oven (220°) for about 5 minutes.

Remove from the oven and transfer the 'package' to a serving dish. Open out the silver foil to reveal the pasta.

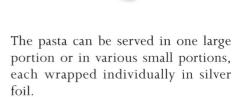

The pasta can be served in one large portion or in various small portions, each wrapped individually in silver foil.

LINGUINE
WITH SCAMPI
AND LEMON

◆

400 g linguine, 400 g medium size scampi, 1 lemon, 1 clove garlic, 1 bunch parsley, red chilli pepper, extra-virgin olive oil, salt.

To enjoy the flavour of this first course at its best, the sauce should be prepared at the time, that is while you are cooking the linguine. Clean and wash the scampi, then dry them and cut them in two lengthways. Heat plenty of oil in a large saucepan, flavouring it with the crushed garlic clove. As soon as the garlic begins to colour, remove it and drop in the scampi. Salt, season with a pinch of chilli pepper, and cook for about ten minutes, turning the shellfish over from time to time.

Cook the linguine in plenty of boiling salted water, draining them while they are still *al dente*, then tip them into the saucepan with the scampi. Sprinkle with the juice of the lemon, finely-sliced strips of the peel (yellow part only), and a handful of finely-chopped parsley. Mix carefully, allowing the flavours to blend, and serve piping hot.

MALLOREDDUS
WITH SWORDFISH SAUCE

◆

400 g malloreddus (recipe on page 133), 2 slices of swordfish, 500 g ripe tomatoes, 25 g salted capers, 1 small onion, 2 garlic cloves, 1 bay leaf, a few basil leaves, 1/2 glass of dry white wine, extra-virgin olive oil, salt, pepper.

This traditional Sardinian pasta goes well with fish sauce but it is generally eaten dry and is therefore best when prepared a few days before.

Clean the swordfish and cut into small cubes, around 2 cm square. Plunge the tomatoes into hot water, skin, remove their seeds and chop finely. Sauté a mixture of chopped onion and garlic in a few spoonfuls of oil and as soon as it becomes transparent, add the fish and, a few minutes later, the white wine. As soon as the wine has almost completly evaporated, add the chopped tomatoes. Add salt, freshly ground pepper, the bay leaf, and the capers which have been rinsed and then dried. Allow to cook over a

moderate heat for about twenty minutes, sprinkle with some chopped basil and turn off the heat.

Cook the pasta in plentiful salted water, drain when *al dente* and mix with half the sauce. Garnish with the remaining sauce and serve.

MALTAGLIATI
WITH CALAMARI
AND VEGETABLES

◆

400 g packet or home-made maltagliati (recipe on page 138), 300 g squid, 3 sprigs black salsify, 200 g ripe tomatoes, 2 large potatoes, 1 clove garlic, 1 small bunch parlsey, chilli powder, extra-virgin olive oil, salt.

Prepare the maltagliati by making a dough, using the basic recipe: divide the dough into strips measuring roughly 1.5 x 6-7 cm: precise measurements are not important. (The name of the pasta means 'cut badly'). Allow to dry on a floured tea-cloth. Plunge the tomatoes into hot water, remove the skin and seeds and chop roughly. Clean the fish, cut into strips and sauté in a few spoonfuls of oil. After a few minutes, add the chopped tomatoes. Continue to cook and a few minutes before removing from the heat, add salt, a little chilli powder and a mixture of chopped parsley and garlic.

Bring to the boil a pot of salted water and cook the potatoes, cut into slices of around 1/2 centimetre thick, and the black salsify which has been cleaned and cut into slices. After 5 minutes add the maltagliati. Drain the pasta and vegetables together and transfer to the pot with the sauce. Toss for a few seconds, mixing well. Turn off the heat, drizzle with oil and serve.

ORECCHIETTE
WITH SARDINES

◆

400 g orecchiette (recipe on page 135), 200 g sardines, 20 g pine-nuts, 1 ladle of tomato sauce, 1 anchovy fillet in oil, 1 clove garlic, 1 leek, 1 small bunch parsley, 1/4 teaspoon saffron, 1/2 chilli pepper, extra-virgin olive oil, pepper.

Clean the sardines, remove the bones and cut into slices. Prepare a mixture of chopped leek, garlic, chilli pepper, a little parsley and the anchovy fillet and sauté in oil. Add the sardines and allow to turn golden; add the pine-nuts, the tomato sauce and the saffron. Continue to cook over a low heat.
Cook the pasta, drain and transfer to the pot with the sauce. Sauté for a few minutes. Turn off the heat, garnish with the chopped parsley and serve immediately.

46

PASTA
WITH TWAITE FILLETS

◆

400 g pasta (any short pasta will do), 8 twaite fillets in oil, 1 small onion, 2 cloves garlic, 300 g fresh tomato sauce, 1 small bunch parsley, about ten black olives, 2 dessertspoons capers, paprika, extra-virgin olive oil, butter, salt.

Heat some oil and a knob of butter; add the chopped onion and the whole cloves of garlic, the twaite fillets, chopped capers, stoned olives and the fresh tomato sauce. Allow to cook for about ten minutes, then add the salt and the chopped parsley and a pinch of paprika. In a pot boil the pasta in salted water, drain when *al dente*, mix with the sauce and serve.

PASTA
WITH SARDINES,
SICILIAN STYLE

◆

400 g maccheroncini, 350 g fresh sardines, 200 g wild fennel, 80 g anchovies in oil, 30 g pine-nuts, 30 g raisins, 2 cloves of garlic, 5 dessertspoons extra-virgin olive oil, 1 dessertspoon chopped parsley, 1 dessertspoon breadcrumbs, saffron, chilli powder, salt, pepper.

Clean the sardines, wash and allow to dry on a tea-cloth. Cook the fennel for a few minutes in a little salted water; drain and dice. Steep the raisins in lukewarm water for 15 minutes.
Crush the garlic and sauté in a few spoonfuls of oil over a low heat. As soon as the garlic begins to colour, remove and add the sardines. Brown on both sides; add the fennel, the drained raisins, the pine-nuts, the chopped parsley, breadcrumbs, salt and chilli powder.
Continue cooking, moving the pot by the handles so as to shift the sauce without breaking the fish; when the sardines are cooked, remove from the pot and lay aside.
Add the anchovies in oil to the pot with a pinch of saffron diluted in a little water. Allow to cook for a few

minutes until the anchovies melt. Cook the maccheroncini in salted water (preferibly the water used to cook the fennel). Drain when al dente and place a layer in an oven dish, alternating with the sauce and the sardines. Finish with a layer of pasta and a layer of sauce. Bake in the oven at 200°C for around 20 minutes. Serve piping hot.

PENNE WITH CAVIAR AND VODKA

◆

400 g penne, 1 small jar caviar, 2-3 small glasses vodka, 1 glass single cream, butter, salt, pepper.

In a pot melt a large knob of butter in the vodka, and allow to evaporate a little. Add the caviar, cream, salt and pepper; remove from the heat as soon as the sauce is warm. In the meantime, cook the penne in plentiful salted water, drain when al dente. Flavour with the vodka and caviar sauce, mixing carefully so as not to break the fish eggs.

PENNE WITH SALMON AND WALNUTS

◆

400 g penne, 200 g sliced smoked salmon, 10 walnuts, 50 g peeled pistachios, 1 small onion, 1 egg yolk, cognac, extra-virgin olive oil, salt, freshly-ground pepper.

Chop the onion finely, and the walnuts and pistachios more roughly, then sauté all together in a large saucepan in a few spoonfuls of oil. After a few minutes pour over a little cognac and let it evaporate, then add the salmon cut into small strips and a twist of freshly-ground pepper. Allow the flavours to blend for a few moments, then turn off the heat. In a large serving-bowl mix the egg yolk with a few spoonfuls of oil and a pinch of salt, then tip in the pasta (boiled, and drained while it is still al dente), pour over the salmon sauce, and mix all the ingredients thoroughly before serving.

A variation on this recipe substitutes the egg yolk with a quarter litre of fresh pouring cream.

PENNE AND PRAWNS IN FOIL

◆

400 g penne, 150 g shelled prawns, 100 g smoked ham in one slice, 150 g fresh peas, shelled, 1 small onion, dry white wine, extra-virgin olive oil, salt, pepper.

Wash the prawns and sauté in a few spoonfuls of oil. Add the wine, then the finely chopped onion, the ham cut into cubes and the peas; add salt, pepper and the peas, (adding, if necessary, a ladle of hot water). Boil the pasta in salted water and drain when *al dente*. Drizzle with oil and then add to the peas and prawns. Transfer to a sheet of silver foil and close the foil. Bake in a hot oven (180°C) for about ten minutes. Serve with the silver foil opened to reveal the pasta.

This pasta can be served as one large serving or several small ones, each individually wrapped in foil.

the squid. When the sauce has thickened, break the ink sacs into the pot with a handful of chopped parsley, salt and chilli powder. Allow the flavours to blend. Cook the spaghetti in salted water, drain when *al dente* and add to the sauce.

You can make a similar dish without the tomatoes: use instead some white wine and a few ladles of warm stock to flavour the squid.

SPAGHETTI
WITH SQUID INK

◆

400 g spaghetti, 400 g baby squid, a few ink sacs, 5 ripe tomatoes (optional), 1 clove garlic, 1 sprig parsley, extra virgin olive oil, salt, chilli pepper.

Clean the squid, removing the bones, eyes and the ink sacs. Take care not to break the sacs because they have to be used later. Wash the squid carefully, then chop roughly. Sauté some crushed garlic in a few spoonfuls of oil, then add the squid and a ladle of warm water and cook for 15 minutes. Skin the tomatoes and remove the seeds. Chop roughly and add to

SPAGHETTI
ALLA CHITARRA
WITH RAZOR CLAMS
(OR CLAMS, DATE MUSSELS, VENUS CLAMS)

◆

500 g spaghetti alla chitarra (recipe on page 136), 1 kg razor clams (or clams, date mussels, or Venus clams), 800 g ripe tomatoes, 3 cloves garlic, a small bunch of parsley, 1/2 glass dry white wine, extra-virgin olive oil, salt, 1 chilli pepper.

Wash the razor clams and allow them to open in a pot with the wine over a rapid heat. Separate the molluscs from the shell (keep some whole for decoration) and filter the liquid.

Sauté some crushed garlic and chopped chilli pepper in a few spoonfuls of oil, add the tomatoes (skinned, with their seeds removed and roughly chopped) and salt and allow to cook for about 15 minutes. Dilute the sauce with the cooking liquid of the razor clams and after 10 minutes, add the molluscs which have been cut into small pieces.

Cook for a further 5 minutes. In the meantime cook the spaghetti in

plentiful salted water and drain when *al dente*. Remove the sauce from the heat, mix in the spaghetti and serve sprinkled with chopped parsley and garnished with the whole razor clams.

This recipe works just as well with any available shellfish, or a mixture of more than one type.

SPAGHETTI
WITH LOBSTER

◆

400 g spaghetti, 1 medium-sized lobster, 250 g tomato purée, 2 cloves garlic, 1 small bunch parsley, extra-virgin olive oil, salt, freshly ground pepper.

Boil the lobster for a few minutes in salted water, drain, remove the shell and cut the meat into pieces. In a pot sauté the garlic clove in a little oil, add the lobster and cook for a few minutes before adding the tomato purée, chopped parsley and salt. Cook over a low heat. In the meantime boil

the pasta in plentiful salted water, drain when *al dente* and serve with the lobster sauce and some freshly ground pepper.

SPAGHETTI
AND SEAFOOD
BAKED IN FOIL

◆

400 g spaghetti, 500 g shellfish (mussels and clams), 200 g squid, 4 small scampi, 4 prawns, 300 g ripe, mature tomatoes, basil, a small onion, dry white wine, extra-virgin olive oil, salt, 1 small chilli pepper.

Clean the various types of fish. Allow the mussels and clams to open in a pot with half a glass of white wine. As they open, separate the molluscs from the shell (leave a few whole for garnish); when you have finished, filter the cooking juices and lay to one side.

Plunge the tomatoes into hot water, skin them, remove the seeds and chop roughly. In a large pot soften the finely chopped onion in a few spoonfuls of oil; when the onion is transparent add the tomatoes. Add the chopped squid and after 10 minutes, the scampi and prawns. Add the liquid from the mussels and clams, adjust the seasoning, add the chilli and continue to cook for about 10 minutes. Add the mussels and clams to the sauce, allow the flavours to blend, and turn off the heat.

Boil the spaghetti in plentiful salted water; drain when *al dente* and mix carefully in the sauce, together with a sprinkling of chopped basil. Lay the spaghetti on the foil, making sure that

49

the pasta is well covered by the scampi and whole prawns. Pinch the edges of the foil together, without allowing the foil to stick to the pasta and cook in a hot oven (180°C) for 5 minutes.

Serve with the foil open. This dish can be served as one large portion or several small portions, each individually wrapped in foil.

SPAGHETTI
WITH ANCHOVIES
AND TRUFFLES

◆

400 g spaghetti, 4 medium-sized black truffles, 4 salted anchovies, 1 clove garlic, extra-virgin olive oil, salt, white pepper.

Wash the anchoves carefully under running water and remove the bones. Clean the truffles, removing the earth completely and pound in a mortar. Heat a little oil in a pot, add the anchovies and allow them to melt, add the crushed garlic and the truffles, salt and pepper. Do not fry the mixture. In the meantime bring to the boil a pot of salted water, add the spaghetti, cook and drain when *al dente*. Flavour with the anchovy and truffle sauce and serve.

SPAGHETTI
WITH FRESH ANCHOVIES

◆

400 g spaghetti, 250 g fresh anchovies, 1/2 lemon, 2 cloves garlic, 1 small bunch parsley, small red pepper, 40 g breadcrumbs, extra-virgin olive oil, salt.

This sauce can be prepared very quickly and requires just a little work to clean the fish. This is done by discarding the head, the tail and the backbone; then wash the anchovies carefully in running water, dry and place in a pot with some chopped garlic and parsley, breadcrumbs and oil.

Allow to cook over a rapid heat for a few minutes, mixing until the anchovies are soft and the breadcrumbs are golden. Add salt and chilli powder. Drain the pasta when *al dente*, mix with the sauce and drizzle with lemon juice before serving.

SPAGHETTI
WITH CLAMS

400 g spaghetti, 1kg clams, 2 cloves garlic, a small bunch parsley, dry white wine (optional), extra-virgin olive oil, salt, 1 chilli pepper.

Clean the shellfish under cold running water, then steep in salted water for half an hour to get rid of any sand. This is very important and should be done with care as the sauce will not be filtered.

In a pot heat several spoonfuls of oil, 1 chopped garlic clove, the chilli and a little wine if desired; add the clams, cover the pot and allow the clams to open.

In the meantime cook the spaghetti in salted water, drain when *al dente* and transfer to the pot with the clams. Mix over a low heat and sprinkle with a mixture of chopped garlic and parsley. Turn off the heat and serve.

SPAGHETTI
WITH BABY EELS

◆

400 g spaghetti, 200 g fresh baby eels, 1 clove of garlic, 1 sprig sage, 4 dessertspoons of tomato sauce, extra-virgin oil, salt.

In a pot heat several spoonfuls of oil and sauté the sage leaves. Add the eels which have been carefully washed. Do this quickly, being ready with the lid in case the heat makes the eels jump out of the pot. Lower the heat and allow to cook for about 10 minutes. Cook the spaghetti in salted water, drain when *al dente*, transfer to the pot with the eels and mix in the tomato sauce. Mix well, adjust the seasoning and serve.

SPAGHETTI
WITH CLAMS
IN TOMATO SAUCE

◆

400 g spaghetti, 500 g clams, 500 g tomato pulp, 2 cloves garlic, a small bunch parsley, 1/2 glass of extra-virgin olive oil, salt, small chilli pepper.

Wash the clams carefully and leave for half an hour in salted water so as to remove any sand. In a large pot heat the oil with the garlic cloves and as soon as they begin to colour, remove and add the tomato pulp. After a few minutes over a rapid heat, lower the heat, add salt and the chilli pepper. When the sauce has thickened, add the clams.
Boil the spaghetti in plentiful salted water, drain when *al dente* and mix with the clam sauce and a sprinkling of

chopped parsley, mixing for a few minutes over the heat to allow the flavours to blend.

BLACK TAGLIATELLE
WITH KING PRAWNS

400 g black tagliatelle (recipe on page 138), 8 king prawns, 1 clove garlic, 1 small bunch parsley, 1 glass dry white wine, extra-virgin olive oil, salt.

Prepare the pasta dough and colour it as described on page 133. Sauté the shelled prawns in oil and flavour with some chopped parsley and garlic and a pinch of salt. Add some white wine and cook over a rapid heat for three minutes.
Boil the pasta in plentiful salted water, drain when *al dente* and transfer to the pot with the sauce. Mix carefully for a few minutes, remove from the heat and serve piping hot, garnishing with the remaining finely chopped parsley.

TAGLIATELLE
WITH ANCHOVIES
AND BREADCRUMBS

◆

400 g tagliatelle (recipe on page 138), 6 salted anchovies, 25 g pine-nuts, 3 cloves of garlic, parsley, 4 generous dessertspoons stale breadcrumbs, 1/2 glass extra-virgin olive oil, salt, chilli powder.

Clean the salt and bones from the anchovies, using a knife and a damp cloth. Heat some oil in a pan, flavour

with crushed garlic (removing as soon as it begins to colour) and a little chilli powder. Add the anchovies and allow to cook with some chopped parsley and pine-nuts.

In a non-stick saucepan toast the breadcrumbs, turning them with a spoon (they should turn golden but not be allowed to become too brown). Boil the pasta in plentiful salted water and drain when *al dente*. Mix with the anchovies and half the breadcrumbs. Transfer to a serving dish. Serve the remaining breadcrumbs on the side, to be sprinkled on the individual portions like grated Parmesan.

lowed to soften at room temperature and cut into little pieces; add salt, pepper. Turn off the heat but keep the sauce warm. Open the scallops, separate the fish from the shells; clean and discard the inedible parts; separate the meat from the roe. Heat the remaining butter in a pan with a clove of garlic (remove as soon as it begins to colour) and sauté the scallops; after a few minutes add the vermouth and allow to evaporate. Turn off the heat, adjust the seasoning, sprinkle with chopped parsley and keep warm. Boil the tagliatelle and drain when *al dente*. Mix the pasta into the butter sauce and garnish with the scallops.

TAGLIATELLE WITH SCALLOPS

◆

400 g black tagliatelle (recipe on page 138), 12 scallops, 1 shallot, 1 clove garlic, 1 small bunch parsley, 2 dl. fish stock, 1 dl. single cream, 1/2 glass of dry vermouth, 1 dl. dry white wine, 120 g butter, salt, pepper.

Prepare the pasta dough and colour it as described on page 133. Chop the shallot finely and allow it to soften over the heat with the wine and fish stock. Cook until the liquid is reduced by half, add the cream and, stirring continuously, thicken the sauce over a low heat. Add 100 g butter which has been al-

TAGLIATELLE WITH TROUT

◆

400 g tagliatelle (recipe on page 138), 250 g trout fillets, 4 skinned tomatoes, 3 zucchini, 1 small onion, dry white wine, extra-virgin olive oil, salt, pepper.

Sauté the finely chopped onion in a little olive oil, add the trout fillets cut into strips and cover with white wine. Allow to evaporate, then add the tomatoes cut into pieces and the zucchini cut into fine disks. Season with

54

salt and pepper and continue to cook over a low heat. In the meantime boil the tagliatelle in plentiful salted water, drain when *al dente* and serve mixed with the trout.

TAGLIOLINI
WITH CAVIAR

◆

400 g tagliolini (*recipe on page 138*), 1 small jar caviar or lumpfish roe, juice of 1 lemon, 1.5 dl. single cream, 80 g butter, salt, freshly ground pepper.

Transfer the caviar to a bowl and add a few drops of lemon juice. Soften the butter at room temperature, chop into little pieces and mix in a large serving bowl with the cream which has been slightly warmed.
Boil the tagliolini and drain when *al dente*. Transfer to the serving dish and mix carefully with the butter and cream, mix in the caviar and some freshly ground pepper.

TAGLIOLINI
WITH SALMON

◆

400 g tagliolini (*recipe on page 138*) 150 g smoked salmon, 1 clove garlic, 1 lemon, 1 cup of fresh single cream, 30 g butter, salt, freshly ground white pepper.

Heat the butter in a saucepan and flavour with the garlic clove; transfer to a large pot and remove the garlic. Heat the pot and add the cream, the chopped salmon, a little grated lemon rind (only the yellow part), a

pinch of salt and mix with care. In the meantime boil the tagliolini in salted water, drain when *al dente* and transfer to the pot with the salmon sauce. Mix for a few minutes over the heat, add a little more butter if necessary and some freshly ground pepper.

TAGLIOLINI
WITH BOTTARGA

◆

400 g tagliolini (*recipe on page 138*), 3 slices of bottarga, 1/2 clove garlic, 1 small bunch parsley, the juice of 1/2 lemon, extra-virgin olive oil, pepper.

Bottarga is salted mullet roe and looks like a kind of hard greyish-brown salami. It can be used in thin slices for the preparation of canapés or grated like Parmesan over a plate of pasta. The following recipe suggests another way to use bottarga as a garnish for pasta. Boil the pasta in plentiful salted water and in the meantime sauté the bottarga in 3 dessertspooons of oil and a little of the water from the pasta; as soon as the bottarga has melted add the juice of a lemon.
Drain the tagliolini when *al dente* and mix into the bottarga,

sprinkle with pepper and a mixture of chopped parsley and garlic.

TROFIE
WITH SQUID

◆

400 g trofie (recipe on page 136), 400 g squid, 1 cup of tomato sauce, 1 sprig basil, 1 small onion, 1 clove garlic, 1 glass dry white wine, 1/2 chilli pepper, extra-virgin olive oil, salt.

Skin and remove the bone from the squid, wash in running water and remove the tentacles. Cut the body into strips. In some oil sauté a mixture of sliced onion, garlic and chilli powder. Add the strips of squid and the tentacles which have been diced and salted. Add the white wine; when it has evaporated add the tomato sauce. Continue to cook over a low heat.
Cook the pasta in plentiful salted water, drain and transfer to the pan with the sauce. Toss for a couple of minutes, turn off the heat. Sprinkle with the chopped fresh basil and serve.

TROFIE
WITH ANCHOVY SAUCE

◆

400 g trofie (recipe on page 136), 4 anchovy fillets in oil, 1 white onion, 1 glass dry white wine, 1 sprig basil, 1 ripe tomato, extra-virgin olive oil, 1/2 red chilli pepper.

Mash the anchovies with a fork. Chop the onion and the chilli and sauté in the oil. Add the anchovies and some white wine and allow to evaporate. Plunge the tomatoes into hot, slightly salted water, skin them and remove their seeds, cut into strips.
Cook the pasta and drain when *al dente*. Transfer to a large serving bowl. Add the anchovies and raw tomatoes, a little more extra-virgin olive oil, some basil leaves and serve.

VERMICELLI
WITH SEAFOOD

◆

400 g vermicelli, 500 g mussels and clams, 200 g fresh lobster meat, 4-5 small scampi, 4-5 king prawns, 500 g ripe, firm tomatoes, 1 small onion, 1 handful basil leaves, 1/2 glass of dry white wine, extra-virgin olive oil, salt, chilli powder

Clean the various types of seafood: rinse the shells and steep in salted water to eliminate any lingering sand. Do not remove the shells. Heat some white wine in a pot and add the mussels and clams; as they open, remove the molluscs from the shell (leave a few for garnish); when you have finished, filter the liquid in the pot and keep to one side. Plunge the tomatoes into hot water, skin them, remove the seeds and chop roughly.
In a large pot sauté the finely chopped onion in a few spoonfuls of oil; add the tomatoes and later the scampi and prawns. After a few minutes add the lobster meat cut into slices. Add the liquid from the mussels and clams, adjust the salt and flavour with chilli powder.
After about 10 minutes add the clams and mussels; allow the flavours to

blend; turn off the heat. In the meantime boil the vermicelli in plentiful salted water; drain when *al dente* and mix carefully into the sauce with a sprinkling of fresh basil.

You can also serve the vermicelli baked in foil. In this case do not allow the pasta to dry in the sauce; after mixing it with the fish, lay it on a sheet of silver foil, making sure that the pasta is well covered by the scampi and whole prawns, close the foil, pinching it round the edges but leaving a little space between the food and the foil. Bake in a hot oven (180°C) for about five minutes.

Serve with the foil open. You can make one large portion or several small portions, individully wrapped in foil.

and wine over a rapid heat. Separate the molluscs from the shells (keeping some to one side) and filter the liquid in the pot. Heat several dessertspoons of oil in a pot, add a mixture of crushed garlic and chilli powder, add the tomatoes (first skin them, remove their seeds and roughly chop) and allow to cook for 15 minutes. Dilute the sauce with the cooking juices of the razor clams and after 10 minutes add the shellfish cut into pieces. Remove from the heat after 5 minutes. Cook the vermicelli in salted water, drain when *al dente* and mix with the sauce. Sprinkle with chopped parsley, mix well, garnish with the whole shellfish. The recipe can be used with all types of shellfish (clams, etc,)

VERMICELLI
WITH RAZOR CLAMS

◆

400 g vermicelli, 1 kg razor clams, 800 g ripe tomatoes, 3 cloves garlic, 1 small bunch parsley, dry white wine, extra-virgin olive oil, salt, chilli powder.

Wash the razor clams well and allow them to open in a pot with a little oil

PASTA WITH VEGETABLES, CHEESE, WINE...

BIGOLI
ALLA PUTTANESCA

◆

400 g bigoli (recipe on page 137), 500 g toma-to pulp, 2 dessertspoons salted capers, 100 g black olives, 2 cloves garlic, 1 small bunch parsley, 2 salted anchovies, extra-virgin olive oil, salt, chilli pepper.

Rinse the capers in running water, re-move the stones from the olives, clean the salt and bones from the an-chovies. Heat some oil in a pan, add the tomatoes, the capers, olives and anchovies.
Cook over a rapid heat for about 10-15 minutes, stirring frequently. Just before turning off the heat check the season-ing, add a little chilli powder and sprinkle with finely chopped parsley. Boil the bigoli in plentiful salted water, drain when al dente and mix well with the sauce before serving.

BIGOLI
WITH FENNEL

◆

400 g bigoli (recipe on page 137), 150 g tomato purée, 2 fennel hearts, 1 onion, 1 bunch parsley, grated Parmesan, extra-virgin olive oil, salt.

Wash the fennel, cut into quarters and blanch in boiling salted water. Chop the onion and parsley and sauté in a little oil over a low heat. As soon as the onion is transparent, add the chopped fennel and allow to cook for 10 min-utes. Add the purée, a pinch of salt and continue to cook with the lid on until the fennel is tender and well blended into the sauce. Cook the bigoli in salt-ed water, drain when al dente, and then transfer to a large serving bown. Mix in the hot sauce, drizzle with oil and sprinkle with Parmesan.

BUCATINI
ALLA BOSCAIOLA

◆

400 g bucatini, 500 g fresh mushrooms, 300 g tomato pulp, 1 clove garlic, 1 small bunch parsley, 1 dessertspoon pine-nuts, 70 g speck cut into thick slices, 1/2 glass of dry white wine, extra-virgin olive oil, salt, pepper.

How you clean the mushrooms will depend on the kind you use. Remove the earth from the heads and also the stems with a damp cloth; if they are large cut them into slices then sauté in a pot with oil and chopped garlic. Al-low to brown, add the wine and as soon as it has evaporated, add the tomato and season with salt and pep-per. Lower the heat and continue cooking in a covered pot for about 15 minutes.
In the meantime cut the speck into cubes and brown in a little oil with the pine-nuts and chopped parsley. Add the speck to the mushrooms, allow the flavours to blend, then mix in the pasta which has been cooked until it is al dente and then drained.

59

BUCATINI
WITH ONION

◆

400 g bucatini, 3 large onions, thyme, red chilli pepper, grated Parmesan, extra-virgin olive oil, salt.

Slice the onion and allow to stew in oil over a low heat, taking care that it doesn't stick.

Just before the onion is completely cooked add a pinch of thyme, one of chilli powder and one of salt. Boil the pasta in plentiful salted water, drain when *al dente* and mix with the sauce and a little oil.

CAVATIEDDI
WITH ROCKET AND TOMATO

◆

400 g cavatieddi (recipe on page 133), 500 g tomato pulp, 300 g rocket, 1 clove garlic, extra-virgin olive oil, mature ricotta, salt, chilli pepper.

Skin the tomatoes by plunging them first into hot water, remove the seeds and chop. Heat the oil and flavour with crushed garlic cloves, add the tomatoes

and allow to cook over a low heat for about 15 minutes, stirring from time to time.

Wash the rocket and parboil in boiling salted water for a few minutes. Use the same water to cook the cavatieddi.

Drain when *al dente* and transfer to the pan with the sauce, mixing with the chopped rocket, a sprinkling of grated ricotta and a pinch of chilli powder. Mix carefully and serve.

FARFALLE
WITH LEMON

◆

400 g farfalle (butterfly-shaped pasta) the juice of one and a half lemons, (if the lemon is very juicy, one will do), 1 bunch basil and chives, 1 glass cream, 50 g butter, salt, pepper.

This is an extremely tasty dish which is very quick and easy to make. Cut the butter into pieces and allow to soften out of the fridge. Mix in a large serving dish with the lemon juice and cream to obtain a soft creamy sauce. Flavour with salt, pepper and finely chopped aromatic herbs.

Boil the farfalle in plentiful salted water, drain when *al dente*; transfer to the serving dish with the lemon butter sauce and mix carefully before serving.

FARFALLE
WITH CHEESE
AND MUSHROOMS

◆

400 g farfalle, 100 g fontina cheese, 50 g grated Parmesan, 50 g grated gruyère, 250 g fresh

and mix into the sauce. Sprinkle with a little finely chopped parsley, mix over the heat for a few minutes more before serving.

FARFALLE
WITH PEPPERS

◆

400 g farfalle, 40 g red and yellow peppers, 400 g ripe, firm tomatoes, 2 cloves garlic, a few leaves of basil, 50 g salted capers, extra-virgin olive oil, salt, chilli powder.

Clean the peppers, removing the seeds and filaments, place them on an oiled tray in a hot oven to allow them to soften and (with a bit of patience) remove the scorched outer film. Cut the peppers into strips, conserving any cooking liquid. Heat a few dessertspoons of oil with the crushed garlic; as soon as it begins to brown, remove it and add the peppers with their sauce. Cook for a few minutes, then add the tomatoes (first skin them, remove the seeds and roughly chop). After about ten minutes over a rapid heat add the capers, which have been rinsed under running water and then dried, add some salt and, a minute or two before turning off the heat, a pinch of chilli powder and some crushed basil leaves.
Boil the farfalle in plentiful salted water, drain, and serve with the sauce.

FUSILLI
WITH FOUR CHEESES

◆

400 g fusilli (curly pasta) 100 g sweet gorgonzola, 100 g fontina, 100 g gruyère, 100 g ta-

61

mush-
rooms,
25 g dried
mushrooms, 2
shallots,   4
firm, ripe toma-
toes,   1   small
bunch parsley, 1
dessertspoon cream,
white wine, extra virgin
olive oil, salt, pepper.

Steep the dried mushrooms; clean the fresh ones carefully using a damp cloth and slice. Dice the shallots and soften in a pan with oil; as they begin to colour add the fresh mushrooms and sauté for a few minutes. Add a little wine and as soon as it evaporates, add the chopped dried mushrooms and the strained water used to steep them. Plunge the tomatoes into hot water, skin them, remove the seeds and chop them; add to the mushrooms with salt and pepper. Continue to stir, allow to cook over a moderate heat for around 30 minutes – if necessary dilute with a little stock or hot salted water. In a large bowl mix the grated cheeses and the fontina cheese cut into little cubes with the cream and about ten minutes before turning off the heat, add to the mushrooms.
In the meantime boil the pasta in plentiful salted water, drain when *al dente*

leggio, milk, 1/2 glass cream, grated Parmesan, salt, pepper.

In a small non-stick saucepan melt the gorgonzola, fontina, taleggio and gruyère cut into little cubes together with a little milk and keep stirring over a low heat. Dilute the sauce with cream and flavour with salt, Parmesan and freshly ground pepper. Warm the saucepan, stirring continuously to obtain a fluid creamy sauce.

In the meantime, cook the pasta, drain when al dente and mix into the cheese. Serve sprinkled with grated Parmesan.

FUSILLI
WITH BROAD BEANS

◆

400 g fusilli, 400 g fresh broad beans, 400 g ripe, firm tomatoes, 2 cloves garlic, a few basil leaves, extra virgin olive oil, salt, chilli powder.

Sauté the chopped garlic in a pan in a few dessertspoons of oil. Clean the broad beans discarding the black eye, then tip them into the pot with the garlic. Allow the flavours to blend then add the tomatoes (first plunge them into hot water to skin, then remove the seeds and chop).
Add salt and a pinch of chilli powder and continue cooking over a moderate heat, adding hot water from time to time. Prior to turning off the heat add the crushed basil leaves. Boil the pasta in plentiful salted water, then drain when al dente and add to the broad bean sauce.

FUSILLI
WITH POMEGRANATE
AND ENDIVE

◆

400 g fusilli, 400 g endive, 2 pomegranates, 150 g ricotta, extra-virgin olive oil, salt, pepper.

Clean the endive and cut into strips. Boil in salted water with the pasta. At the same time, in a warmed serving dish, mix the ricotta with two spoonfuls of the water from the pasta pot; add salt, pepper and blend the pomegranate seeds into the mixture.
Drain the pasta and endive and transfer to the serving bowl, mixing carefully with the ricotta and pomegranate. Drizzle with extra-virgin olive oil.

LINGUINE
WITH SWEETENED
CAULIFLOWER

400 g linguine, 1 onion, 1 medium-sized cauliflower, 80 g raisins, 80 g pine-nuts, salt, pepper, extra-virgin olive oil, grated Parmesan (optional).

Steep the raisins in lukewarm water. In the meantime, clean the cauliflower, boil in a little salted water, drain when still very firm and cut into small pieces. In a pan sauté the chopped onion in a little oil and af-

ter a few minutes add the cauliflower and pine-nuts. Drain the raisins and squeeze out the moisture. Together with a little of the water used for steeping, add them to the cauliflower and onion. Add a pinch of salt and one of pepper and allow to cook over a moderate heat. Boil the pasta in plentiful salted water and when *al dente*, drain and transfer to a large serving bowl with half of the sauce. Bring to the table and drizzle the individual portions with the remaining sauce. Serve some grated Parmesan on the side.

MACCHERONCINI PRIMAVERA

◆

400 g small wholewheat maccheroncini, 1 kg asparagus, 300 g fresh ricotta cheese, 2 eggs, a little milk, 100 g grated Parmesan cheese, extra-virgin olive oil, salt, chilli pepper.

Clean the asparagus carefully and cook them for about 5 minutes in salted, boiling water. Drain them thoroughly then chop into pieces, eliminating the woody parts, tip them into a large saucepan with a few spoonfuls of oil and sauté lightly.
In a bowl, blend the ricotta with a few spoonfuls of milk, a pinch of salt, and chilli pepper to taste, beating until you have a smooth, soft paste.
To cook the pasta, bring a large saucepan with the asparagus cooking water to the boil, adding more water if required. Drop in the maccheroncini, cook, and drain while they are still *al dente*.

Oil an ovenproof dish and arrange a first layer of pasta, covering it with grated Parmesan cheese and a trickle of oil. Sprinkle over half the asparagus and spread with half the ricotta cream. Repeat the layers of maccheroncini, asparagus and ricotta, then spread a final layer of maccheroncini, pouring over it the eggs beaten with a pinch of salt, one of chilli pepper, and a couple of spoons of grated Parmesan. Finally, brown in the oven for about half an hour before serving.

MALLOREDDUS WITH POTATOES

◆

400 g malloreddus (recipe on page 133), 400 g potatoes, 200 g onions, extra-virgin olive oil, grated pecorino, salt, freshly ground pepper.

The influence of Sardinia is in the pasta as well as this simple, tasty sauce. Remember that this type of pasta is better dry and can therefore be cooked a couple of days before it is required.
Clean the vegetables, cut the potatoes into cubes and slice the onion. Bring to the boil a pot of salted water and add the potatoes. After 15 minutes add the pasta. In the meantime heat some oil in a pan and sauté the finely chopped onion. Drain the potatoes and pasta when the latter is *al dente*. Transfer to the pan with the onion, stir over a moderate heat for a few seconds, add the grated pecorino and some freshly ground pepper. Turn off the heat and serve.

ORECCHIETTE
WITH BROCCOLI

◆

400 g orecchiette (recipe on page 135) 300 g broccoli, 2 cloves garlic, 1 dessertspoon raisins (optional), 2 salted anchovies, grated pecorino, extra-virgin olive oil, salt, chilli powder.

Wash the broccoli carefully and cook in plentiful salted water. Drain when still firm but reserve the water for cooking the pasta. Steep the raisins in lukewarm water.

Heat some olive oil, add the chopped garlic. Clean the salt off the anchovies and blend them into the oil. Add the broccoli and continue to cook the sauce (add a little hot salted water if necessary). Shortly before removing from heat, check the seasoning, flavour with chilli powder and add the pine-nuts and raisins which have been drained and squeezed to eliminate all the moisture.

Cook the orecchiette, drain when *al dente*, mix into the sauce and flavour with pecorino which has been grated or cut into little cubes.

PANSOTTI
WITH WALNUTS

◆

<u>FOR THE PASTA:</u> the recipe is on page 138
<u>FOR THE FILLING:</u> 300 g ricotta, 500 g chard, 500 g preboggion (cabbage head, chard and parsley), 1 bunch of borage, 3 eggs, 50 g Parmesan, nutmeg, salt.
<u>FOR THE SAUCE:</u> walnuts, pine-nuts, 1 garlic clove, extra-virgin olive oil.

Prepare the pasta as described in the recipe, roll out and divide into little 6cm squares. Make the filling: wash, boil and chop the vegetables. In a bowl mix the ricotta, grated Parmesan, eggs, salt and some grated nutmeg; finally add the chopped vegetables. Mix carefully to obtain a smooth stuffing and drop a little into the centre of each pasta square. Fold the pasta over into a triangle, pressing the edges firmly together. Cook the pansotti in boiling salted water and in the meantime, prepare the sauce. Chop the walnuts, pine-nuts and garlic, then pound all together in a mortar, adding enough oil to obtain a consistent, smooth sauce. Allow to rest. Drain the pansotti when *al dente* and transfer to a warmed serving dish. Cover with the nut sauce and serve immediately.

PASTA
WITH RICOTTA

◆

400 g pasta (any short pasta will do), 250 g fresh ricotta, 100 g grated mature ricotta, lard, salt, chilli powder.

Cook the pasta in plentiful salted water and in the meantime prepare the sauce. Melt a little lard in a pot and mix in the fresh ricotta.
Drain the pasta when al dente and mix with the melted ricotta. Sprinkle with grated ricotta and a pinch of chilli powder; mix well before serving.
You can make this recipe more personal by adding aromatic herbs and other ingredients of your choice: oregano, ginger, chopped black olives.

PASTA
WITH CARROTS

400 g pasta (any short pasta will do), salt, 2 onions, 2 cloves of garlic, about ten medium-sized carrots, 2 celery stalks, 1 sprig rosemary, 1 dessert-spoon sesame seeds, extra-virgin olive oil, salt.

Clean the carrots carefully under running water, using a special

brush; allow to dry. Clean the celery. Finely chop the onion and garlic and place in a pot with oil and rosemary. Sauté over a rapid heat.
Slice the carrots lengthwise and finely chop the celery. Add both to the pot, add the sesame seeds, a pinch of salt, and after a few minutes, lower the heat, cover and continue cooking for about 15 minutes, stirring from time to time so the mixture doesn't stick.
Cook the pasta in plentiful salted water; when al dente drain and mix into the sauce. Toss over the heat for a few seconds, The success of this recipe largely depends on the carrots: they should be al dente: cooked, but still firm.

PASTA
WITH LENTILS

◆

400 g wholemeal pasta (any short pasta will do), 200 g whole lentils, 1 carrot, 1 stick of celery, 2 cloves garlic, 2 bay leaves, 1 bunch parsley, red chilli powder, extra-virgin olive oil, salt.

Steep the lentils for 12 hours. Drain, rinse, and cook in plentiful salted water together with the diced celery, diced carrot and bay leaves. Cover the pot and continue to cook over a moderate heat.
When the lentils are almost ready, add the pasta. Remove from the heat when the pasta is al dente. Transfer to a large serving bowl and mix with a sauce prepared with oil, chopped parsley, finely chopped garlic, and chilli

powder cooked for fifteen minutes over a moderate heat.

PASTA WITH PARMESAN AND ZUCCHINI

400 g wholemeal pasta (any short type will do), 800 g zucchini, 1 kg ripe tomatoes, 150 g moz-zarella, a few basil leaves, red chilli powder, grated Parmesan, extra-virgin olive oil, salt.

Wash the zucchini and chop into slices lengthwise. Leave them for about an hour at room temperature or in the sun, then fry in oil. Allow to dry on paper towel. Cook half of the sliced tomatoes in a pot with only a pinch of salt and a few basil leaves. In an oiled ovenproof dish, form a layer of tomato sauce, covered with one of zucchini, slices of mozarella, grated Parmesan and end with a layer of zucchini covered with the last spoonfuls of sauce. Place in a hot oven (180°C) for about half an hour. In the meantime, plunge the remaining tomatoes into hot water, skin them and remove the seeds; cook in the same pot as before with oil, salt and chilli powder. When ready, add to the dish of Parmesan and zucchini, mix and allow to cook for about ten minutes, adding, if necessary, a few spoonfuls of hot water so the mixture doesn't stick. Cook the pasta in salted water, drain and transfer to a serving dish. Cover with the sauce and add a few fresh basil leaves. Serve with grated Parmesan on the side.

PASTA WITH RICOTTA AND ARTICHOKES

400 g pasta (any short pasta will do), 250 g ricotta, 4 artichokes, 1 shallot, 1 clove garlic, a small bunch parsley, 1 lemon, dry white wine, extra-virgin olive oil, grated Parmesan, salt, pepper.

Remove a part of the stem and the sharp point from the outer leaves of the artichokes, cut into fine wedges and steep in water diluted with lemon. Finely chop the shallot and garlic and sauté in several spoonfuls of oil. Drain the artichokes and add to the pot, stirring all the time over a rapid heat. After a few minutes lower the heat and add some white wine. Allow to evaporate. Season with salt and pepper and continue cooking, covered, for around 20 minutes. If necessary add a little hot salted water. Boil the pasta and drain when *al dente*. Transfer to a pot with the sauce, add the crumbled ricotta, a few dessertspoons of Parmesan and a sprinkling of finely chopped parsley. Mix well, allow the cheese to melt a little before turning off the heat. Serve piping hot.

PENNE ALL'ARRABBIATA

◆

400 g penne, 500 g ripe, firm tomatoes, 2 cloves garlic, extra-virgin olive oil, grated pecorino, salt, 1 chilli pepper.

Plunge the tomatoes into hot water, skin, remove the seeds and chop. Sauté the garlic clove in several spoonfuls of oil.

Add the tomatoes and allow the sauce to thicken over a moderate heat, season with salt and the crumbled chilli pepper and cook for a further 20 minutes over a moderate heat. Cook the pasta in plentiful boiling salted water and drain when *al dente*. Mix into the sauce, turn up the heat for a few seconds, sprinkle with grated pecorino. Turn off the heat and serve.

REGINETTE ALLA PARMIGIANA

◆

400 g reginette, 150 g fresh grated Parmesan, a few sage leaes, 1 clove garlic, 100 g butter, nutmeg, salt, pepper.

The sauce is prepared while the pasta is cooking in salted water. Over a low heat, melt the butter, add the sage leaves and the crushed garlic clove. As soon as the butter has melted and is beginning to colour (it should not be allowed to become too brown), remove from the heat and discard the aromatic herbs. Add a few spoonfuls of cooking water

from the pasta to the butter and add the grated Parmesan, mixing well to blend; flavour with a little salt and some nutmeg.

Drain the reginette when *al dente* and transfer to the pot with the Parmesan sauce. Turn up the heat. Stir well to blend in all the ingredients, add a little freshly ground pepper, turn off the heat and serve.

SPAGHETTI WITH VEGETARIAN CARBONARA

400 g spaghetti, 6 zucchini, 1 onion, 1/2 pepper, 1 cabbage leaf, 2 eggs, nutmeg, grated Parmesan, extra-virgin olive oil, salt.

Wash and slice the vegetables; sauté the sliced onion in oil, add the chopped pepper, the cabage leaf and zucchini.

Add salt, cover the pot and allow to cook for a little over 15 minutes. In the meantime boil the pasta. Beat the eggs with a little salt and grated nutmeg.

When the pasta is al dente, drain and transfer to the pot with the vegetables, add the oil and the beaten egg and allow the flavours to blend for about two minutes over a moderate heat. Serve with the grated Parmesan on the side.

SPAGHETTI
WITH GARLIC, OIL
AND CHILLI PEPPER

◆

400 g spaghetti, 4 cloves garlic, 1 glass extra-virgin olive oil, salt, 1 chilli pepper.

Considered something of a 'classic', this recipe is one of the quickest and easiest to prepare and is certain to be a success.
Boil the pasta in plentiful salted water and in the meantime sauté the crushed chilli pepper and the finely chopped garlic in a few spoonfuls of oil in a pan.
For a sauce which is less spicy, discard the chilli from the oil before adding the garlic; if you want the garlic taste to be less pronounced, allow the garlic to flavour the oil but remove it before heating the oil with the chilli.

SPAGHETTI
WITH BRANDY

◆

400 g spaghetti, 4 small glasses brandy, 70 g grated parmesan, 100 g butter, 1 stock cube.

While this recipe seems very unusual, it is really quick to prepare and is very tasty. Cook the pasta in plentiful salted water and in the meantime prepare the sauce: in a non-stick saucepan, over a moderate heat, melt the stock cube in the brandy. Keep stirring with a wooden spoon because the brandy should not be allowed to evaporate completely. Add the butter, which has been allowed to soften at room tem-

perature and cut into pieces, and then the Parmesan.
Drain the spaghetti when *al dente* and mix into the sauce. You can sprinkle with more Parmesan before serving.

SPAGHETTI
WITH TOMATO SAUCE

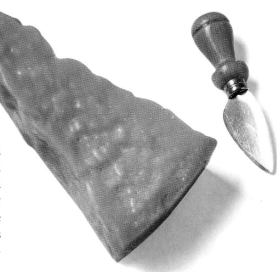

400 g spaghetti, 800 g firm, ripe tomatoes, a few basil leaves, 1 teaspoon sugar, extra-virgin olive oil, salt, chilli powder.

This is probably the most classical of traditional sauces with a tomato base: 'pommarola', considered the sauce *par excellence* for accompanying pasta. Wash the tomatoes, plunge them into boiling water, skin them, remove the seeds and stalks and then pass them through a food mill. If there is too much water, leave the tomatoes on a sloping surface for about 15 minutes to allow the excess liquid to drain off, then cook over a moderate heat with a little oil. Cook until the mixture thickens (about 30 minutes), seasoning with a

pinch of salt and a teaspoon of sugar (this helps to reduce the acid taste of the tomatoes).

Just before turning off the heat add the chilli pepper and crushed basil. Boil the spaghetti and drain when *al dente*, then serve in individual portions, each with a generous amount of sauce and a drizzle of olive oil.

SPAGHETTI ALLA NORMA

◆

400 g spaghetti, 600 g tomato pulp, 3 aubergines, 1 onion, a few basil leaves, 1 large mozzarella, extra-virgin olive oil, salt, chilli powder.

Clean the aubergines and cut into slices about 1cm. thick; sprinkle with salt and leave for two hours on paper towel to eliminate the bitter juices. Rinse, dry well, cut into cubes and fry in oil. Allow to dry on paper towel.

Chop the onion and sauté in several spoonfuls of oil; add the tomatoes, season with salt and chilli powder and allow to thicken over a moderate heat.

Boil the pasta, drain when *al dente*, transfer to a serving bowl, mix with the mozzarella cut into little cubes, the tomato sauce, the fried aubergine and the crushed basil leaves. Mix carefully and serve.

SPAGHETTI WITH AUBERGINE

◆

400 g spaghetti, 3 long aubergines, 2 garlic cloves, 1 small bunch parsley, extra-virgin olive oil, salt.

Wash and dry the aubergines. Cut into quite thick slices, place on a sloping surface (a plate will do) and sprinkle with coarse salt to eliminate the bitter juices. After about two hours rinse, drain well, dry and fry in plentiful oil with a little crushed garlic. When cooked, lay on absorbent paper to drain off excess oil. Cook the spaghetti and when *al dente*, drain, mix with the aubergine in a warmed serving dish and sprinkle with a little chopped parsley. Serve the spaghetti hot.

SPAGHETTI WITH CHICORY

400 g spaghetti, 4 heads of chicory, 1/2 onion, 150 g fontina (optional), 1/2 glass cream, extra-virgin olive oil, nutmeg, salt, pepper.

Wash the chicory carefully and cut into strips. Sauté the finely chopped onion in a few spoonfuls of oil; add the chicory, cover the pot and allow to cook over a low heat. Before turning off the heat, season with salt and a generous amount of freshly ground pepper. In the meantime, boil the spaghetti and drain when *al dente*; transfer to the pot with the chicory. Mix well with the cream and the fontina

cheese cut into little cubes. Sprinkle with grated nutmeg.

SPAGHETTI
WITH PUMPKIN SAUCE

◆

400 g spaghetti, 500 g yellow pumpkin (the bumpy kind is better), 500 g onion, 50 g grated Parmesan, 50 g grated pecorino, 1 glass dry white wine, extra-virgin olive oil, salt, pepper.

Remove the skin from the pumpkin and cut into little cubes. Finely chop the onion and sauté with the pumpkin in oil. Cover the pot and allow to cook over a moderate heat. As soon as the pumpkin is cooked, uncover the pot, season with salt and pepper and add the wine. Turn up the heat and allow the wine to evaporate, stirring continuously and mashing the pumpkin with a wooden spoon.
In the meantime cook the spaghetti in plentiful salted water, drain and transfer to a serving dish.
Add the pasta to the pumpkin sauce

and the grated cheese. Mix together before serving.

SPAGHETTI, CHEESE
AND PEPPER

◆

400 g spaghetti, 150 g grated pecorino, salt, pepper.

Boil the spaghetti in plentiful salted water and drain when *al dente*, reserving a little cooking water. Transfer this water to a large serving bowl, add the pecorino and plenty of freshly ground pepper. Mix well, then fold in the spaghetti. Serve piping hot. In the original recipe, oil or butter is not included in the pasta sauce.

SPAGHETTI
WITH WALNUTS

400 g spaghetti, 400 g walnuts, 1 clove garlic, 1 handful breadcrumbs, 100 g cream, extra-virgin olive oil, salt, nutmeg.

Shell the walnuts and remove the film which covers them by plunging them into boiling water. Pound them in a mortar with the garlic clove and then add the breadcrumbs which have been moistened in some water (or milk) and squeezed dry, and a handful of salt. Use the pestle like a spoon to mix the ingredients together to obtain a smooth cream. In a saucepan, warm the nut mixture over a moderate heat, diluting with the cream and a

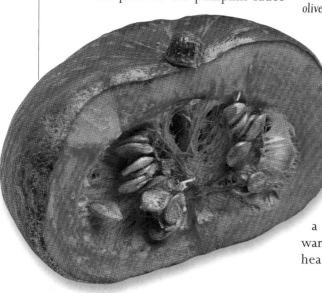

few spoonfuls of oil. Turn off the heat before the sauce boils.

Drain the spaghetti when *al dente* and flavour with the nut sauce. Sprinkle with a little grated nutmeg.

SPAGHETTI
WITH DRIED BROAD BEANS

◆

400 g wholemeal spaghetti, 250 g dried broad beans, 3 tomatoes, 1 onion, gomasho, extra-virgin olive oil, salt.

Steep the dried broad beans for 24 hours. Drain and remove the skins which should come away easily. Cook them in a pot with enough fresh water to cover them (it is important to change the water as the beans expel toxins while steeping), the finely chopped onion, the tomatoes which have been washed and cut into slices.

Cook for about two hours over a low heat in a covered pot. When the beans are cooked and the water has been almost totally absorbed, add oil (four or five dessertspoons) and salt. Boil the pasta, drain it *al dente*, then mix it with the beans. Mix thoroughly, sprinkle with gomashio and serve.

SPAGHETTI
WITH BEAN SAUCE

◆

400 g wholemeal spaghetti, 120 g beans (if possible, white Spanish beans), 10 chives, 1 sprig rosemary, a few bay leaves, 1 teaspoon tarragon, gomasho, extra virgin olive oil, salt.

Steep the beans in cold water with a bay leaf. After about 14 hours drain, rinse and cook in fresh water with the rosemary. When the beans are cooked. pass through a food mill and reduce to a cream, adding a little cooking water if necessary. (The same water can also be used for cooking the pasta). Enrich the bean sauce with oil, salt, the aromatic herbs which have been chopped and mixed together. Cook the spaghetti in plentiful salted water, drain when *al dente* and mix in a large serving bowl with the bean mixture. Sprinkle with gomashio and serve.

SEDANINI
AND ZUCCHINI

◆

400 g sedanini, 500 g zucchini, 1 clove garlic, a bunch parsley or mint, cream (optional), extra virgin olive oil, grated parmesan, salt, pepper.

Clean the zucchini and cut into rounds. Heat some oil in a pan, sauté the sliced garlic and the zucchini. Mix carefully so as not to break the zucchini,

add salt, pepper and sprinkle with chopped parsley or mint.

Cook the pasta in plentiful salted water, drain when al dente and transfer to the pan with the zucchini. Mix the pasta with the sauce, adding a little cream if desired, and serve with grated parmesan.

TAGLIATELLE
WITH ASPARAGUS

◆

400 g tagliatelle (recipe on page 138), 2 bunches of asparagus, 1 dessertspoon lemon juice, nutmeg, 2.5 dl milk, extra-virgin olive oil, salt, pepper.

Clean the apsaragus, slice the tips and the soft part of the stalk and sauté in a few spoonfuls of oil. Add salt, pepper, nutmeg and a little less than 1/2 glass of hot water. Cover and allow to cook over a moderate heat for 15 minutes; as soon as the water has dried up, add the lemon juice.

Cook the asparagus until tender, adding the milk from time to time. Mix the sauce in a blender, heat again and blend in with the cooked tagliatelle.

Wild asparagus can also be used for this dish as long as you are careful to gather it in un-polluted areas, and use only the tenderest parts.

TAGLIATELLE
WITH HERBS

◆

400 g tagliatelle (see basic recipe on page 138), 1 bunch of herbs (including savory, marjoram, basil, parsley, chives and thyme) extra-virgin olive oil, salt.

Prepare the equivalent of a dessertspoon of finely chopped herbs for each person (more savory can be used, while the thyme and chives should be used sparingly). In the meantime, boil the pasta, and drain it while it is still al dente. Sprinkle with the herb mixture, pour over plenty of olive oil, and serve. Obviously fresh herbs give better results, but in the absence of these dried herbs can be used; chop them finely and steep them in oil for about fifteen minutes before use.

TAGLIATELLE
WITH PEAS

◆

400g tagliatelle (see basic recipe on page 138), 500g shelled peas, 400g ripe, firm

tomatoes, 1 onion, 1 carrot, 1 bunch parsley, extra-virgin olive oil, salt, pepper.

Chop the onion and carrot and sauté them in a saucepan in a little oil; stir in the peas and allow the flavours to blend. Plunge the tomatoes in boiling water, peel, seed and chop them, then add to the sauce. Season with salt and pepper and continue cooking, adding a little hot water from time to time. Just before you turn off the heat, add the chopped parsley. Boil the tagliatelle in plenty of salted water, drain while they are still al dente, and stir in half the sauce. Serve with the rest of the sauce spooned over the pasta.

This sauce can also be made without tomatoes, in which case you should use two onions rather than one. Another variation includes the addition of a little cream to the sauce at the end of cooking.

TAGLIATELLE
WITH TALEGGIO CHEESE
AND TRUFFLES

◆

400 g tagliatelle (see basic recipe on page 138), 150 g Taleggio cheese, 1 small black truffle, 1/2 glass cream, dry white wine, butter, grated Parmesan cheese, salt, pepper.

Scrape the rind off the Taleggio without removing it completely, and cut the cheese into small pieces. Warm it gently in a saucepan with a knob of but-

ter and the cream, stirring until the sauce becomes smooth and creamy. Season with salt and pepper.

In the meantime boil the tagliatelle, drain them while they are still al dente, and tip them into the saucepan with the cheese sauce, mixing well. Brush the truffle, and rinse it in a little white wine; grate this over the pasta before serving it with grated Parmesan cheese.

TRENETTE
WITH WHITE CABBAGE

400 g trenette, 500 g white cabbage, 2 carrots, 1 onion, 2 bay leaves, dry white wine, extra-virgin olive oil, salt.

Wash the onion, chop it finely, and sauté it rapidly in a little oil with the bay leaves over a high heat for a few minutes. Add the cleaned and sliced carrots, stirring every so often. In the meantime, clean the white cabbage and slice it very finely, then put it in the pan, cover and simmer with the other vegetables for about twenty minutes over a moderate heat. When the cabbage is soft and the sauce almost cooked, pour over the white wine, let it evaporate, and finish cooking, adjusting salt to taste.

Boil the trenette, drain them while they are still al dente, and tip them in with the vegetables. Keep on the heat for a few more minutes, stirring all the time, then serve piping hot in a soup tureen.

TAGLIOLINI
WITH MASCARPONE

◆

400 g tagliolini (see basic recipe on page 138), 150 g mascarpone cheese, 3 egg yolks, 6-8 dessertspoons of grated Parmesan cheese, grated nutmeg, salt, pepper.

This sauce should be prepared just a few minutes before cooking the pasta. Have the eggs at room temperature, then in a saucepan mix the yolks with the grated Parmesan, a pinch of salt and a grind of fresh pepper, stirring until you have a smooth cream. Place the saucepan over a very low heat, or better still in a double-boiler (or bain-marie) then stirring carefully, add the mascarpone and season with the grated nutmeg. Cook the pasta, drain it while it is still al dente, tip it into the sauce and mix well.
You can give this dish a touch of refinement by garnishing it at the moment of serving with a little lumpfish roe (or real caviar) and a sprinkle of grated lemon peel.

TAGLIOLINI
IN SWEET WINE SAUCE

◆

400 g tagliolini (see basic recipe on page 138), 2 glasses sweet white wine, 150 g speck (smoked raw ham) in a single slice, 150 g cooked ham (in a single slice), 300 g tomato purée, 2 glasses cream, extra-virgin olive oil, grated Parmesan cheese, salt, pepper.

Cut the speck and the cooked ham into thin strips and sauté them in a little oil until they just begin to brown. Pour over the wine, and let it evaporate over a gentle heat. Then add the tomato purée, and

82

as soon as it begins to boil, add the cream. Season with salt and pepper and leave to simmer for about ten minutes.
Boil the tagliolini in plenty of salted water, drain them while they are still al dente, tip them into the sauce, and mix thoroughly. Complete with a sprinkle of grated Parmesan cheese.

TRENETTE WITH PESTO

400 g trenette, 100 g green beans, 2 potatoes, about thirty basil leaves, 1 clove garlic, 1-2 dessertspoons pine-kernels, 1 dessertspoon grated Pecorino cheese, 1 dessertspoon grated Parmesan cheese, extra-virgin olive oil, salt.

Wash and dry the basil leaves, then put them in a stone mortar with the garlic and the pine-kernels (pressing the basil against the sides with circular movements rather than actually pounding it). Continue grinding the ingredients, then add the grated cheeses and a pinch of salt. As soon as you have a smooth paste, add olive oil drop by drop, stirring with the pestle like a spoon, until you have a thick, creamy sauce. If you prefer, the pesto can also be successfully made in a blender.
Peel the dice the potatoes and top and tail the green beans and cut into short lengths. Set the vegetables to boil in plenty of salted water, and as soon as they are par-boiled, add the trenette. When the pasta is still al dente, drain together with the vegetables, and pour

over both the pesto sauce diluted with two dessertspoons of the cooking water. Mix thoroughly, and serve.

VERMICELLI WITH LEEKS

◆

400 g vermicelli, 4 medium size leeks, 1 tomato, 1 dessertspoon tamari sauce, extra-virgin olive oil, salt.

Clean the leeks carefully, removing the harder green parts, and cut into slices of about 1cm. Sauté briefly in a saucepan in a little oil, then cover and leave to simmer over a low heat for about ten minutes. Wash and roughly chop the tomato, and add it to the leeks along with a glass of hot water, the tamari sauce and a pinch of salt. Continue simmering for a further 20 minutes. Cook the pasta, draining it while it is still *al dente*, then pour over the piping hot sauce, mix, and serve immediately.

VERMICELLI IN RAW VEGETABLE SAUCE

◆

400 g vermicelli, 500 g small ripe firm tomatoes, 1 carrot, 1 small onion, 1 clove garlic, basil, extra-virgin olive oil, salt, chilli pepper.

Plunge the tomatoes in boiling water for a few minutes, then peel, seed and chop them. If they are very watery, slice the tomatoes in half and leave them on a sloping surface for about 15 minutes

to let the water drain off before chopping them. Slice the carrot, cut the onion finely into rings and slice the garlic, and put them all in a large bowl together with the tomatoes. Season with a generous dash of oil, a pinch of salt, a pinch of chilli and the chopped basil, and mix thoroughly. Leave the sauce in a cool place for a couple of hours.

Cook the pasta in plenty of boiling salted water, drain it while it is still *al dente*, and then serve with the prepared sauce.

This base recipe can be varied and enriched according to the seasonal availability of fresh vegetables, and the creativity of each individual cook.

ZITE WITH ONION AND BREADCRUMBS

◆

400 g zite, 2 large onions, 2 cloves garlic, oregano, 4 dessertspoons breadcrumbs, 2 glasses white wine, 1 glass extra-virgin olive oil, salt, chilli pepper.

Slice the onions and garlic finely and sauté in a large saucepan with the oil. After a few minutes add the breadcrumbs, frying them lightly, but making sure that the onion does not brown. As soon as the sauce begins to dry, pour over the wine and season with a pinch of oregano, salt, and a little chilli. In the meantime, boil the zite, drain them while they are still *al dente*, and tip them into the pan with the onions and the wine which has not yet completely evaporated. Stir thoroughly over the heat for a few more minutes, adding a little oil if necessary.

BAKED
PASTA

BAKED CANNELLONI

◆

<u>FOR THE PASTA</u>: (*see basic recipe on page 137*)
<u>FOR THE BÉCHAMEL</u>: (*see page 141*)

These are three of the most classic versions of baked cannelloni: with spinach and ricotta, with mincemeat and tomato, and with tuna. They can all be varied and enriched according to taste and to the imaginative flair of the cook. All recipes start with the preparation of the pasta base for the cannelloni following the instructions given, and proceed with the preparation of the béchamel, also following the base recipe.
The different fillings can then be made as follows:

SPINACH AND RICOTTA FILLING

500 g spinach, 250 g ricotta cheese, grated Parmesan cheese, 2 eggs, béchamel (see page 141), butter, grated nutmeg, salt, pepper.

Wash, trim and boil the spinach in a little salted water, then drain and leave to cool. Squeeze it out well, and chop finely. Mash the ricotta thoroughly in a bowl, and mix it with the spinach, egg yolks, and a few spoonfuls of grated Parmesan. Season with salt, pepper and grated nutmeg.
If the mixture is too stiff, add the egg whites or a drop of warm milk, then use the filling to stuff the pasta squares. Roll up the cannelloni, and lay them in an ovenproof dish with a layer of béchamel in the bottom. Pour over the rest of the sauce, then sprinkle with grated Parmesan and dot with a few flakes of butter. Brown in a pre-heated oven at 180°C for about half an hour.

MINCEMEAT AND TOMATO FILLING

◆

300 g minced beef, 100 g tomato pulp, 1 onion, basil, 1/2 glass red wine, béchamel (see page 141, half-quantity), 2 eggs, 100 g grated Parmesan cheese, extra-virgin olive oil, salt. pepper.

In a saucepan, soften the chopped onion in a few spoonfuls of oil, then add the mincemeat, stirring well so that it browns evenly. Pour over the wine, let it evaporate, then season with salt and pepper and add the tomato pulp. Leave to cook for about 30 minutes, adding a few basil leaves before removing from the heat. Let the sauce cool, then blend in the eggs and the Parmesan.
Use the filling to stuff the cannelloni, then arrange them in an ovenproof dish with a thin layer of béchamel in the bottom. Pour over the rest of the sauce, and sprinkle with grated Parmesan, chopped basil and dot with a few flakes of butter. Brown in a pre-heated oven at 180°C for about half and hour.

TUNA FILLING

◆

500 g tuna in oil, 500 g peeled tomatoes, 1 onion, 3 dessertspoons capers, 1 bunch parsley, basil, 1 large Mozzarella cheese, extra-virgin olive oil, butter, salt, pepper.

Chop the tuna, mozzarella and capers very finely, and season with

chopped parsley and basil, and a pinch of salt and pepper. In a saucepan, sauté the chopped onion in a few spoonfuls of oil, then add the peeled and seeded tomatoes, season with salt, and simmer over a low heat for about 30 minutes. Add chopped parsley and pepper before removing from the heat. Stuff the cannelloni with the tuna filling and arrange them in a buttered oven-proof dish. Pour over the tomato sauce and dot with a few flakes of butter. Cook in a pre-heated oven (200°C) for about ten minutes.

CANNELLONI
WITH SALMON

◆

FOR THE PASTA: *(see basic recipe on page 137).*
FOR THE SAUCE: *1 cup béchamel (see page 141), butter.*
FOR THE FILLING: *400 g salmon meat, 2 zucchini, 12 stems asparagus, 1 egg, 100 g ricotta cheese, salt.*

Scald the diced zucchini and the asparagus tips in boiling salted water, then drain them carefully. In the blender, whiz the raw salmon meat, the zucchini, the asparagus tips, the egg and a pinch of salt. Pour the mixture into a bowl, stir in the ricotta and blend thoroughly.
Cook the pasta, drain, and lay to dry on a tea cloth. Place the pasta squares on a floured work-surface, spread over the filling, and roll them up. Arrange the cannelloni in a buttered ovenproof dish, pour over the béchamel and dot with a few flakes of butter. Brown in a pre-heated oven (180°C) for about 15 minutes, then serve.

CANNELLONI
WITH SPINACH AND HAM

◆

FOR THE PASTA: *(see basic recipe on page 137).*
FOR THE SAUCE: *1 ladleful béchamel (see page 141), butter, grated Parmesan cheese.*
FOR THE FILLING: *300 g spinach, 200 g thickly sliced cooked ham, 2 eggs, 150 g Fontina cheese, 50 g butter, grated Parmesan cheese, grated nutmeg, salt.*

Wash and trim the spinach, scald in a little salted boiling water, squeeze, then chop finely. Dice the ham and melt the Fontina cheese gently in a saucepan with the butter. In a bowl, mix together with a wooden spoon the spinach, ham, Fontina, a handful of grated Parmesan, the eggs a pinch of nutmeg and one of salt.
Cook the pasta, drain, and lay to dry on a tea cloth. Place the pasta squares on a floured work-surface, spread over the filling, and roll them up. Arrange the cannelloni in a buttered ovenproof dish, pour over the béchamel, sprinkle with grated Parmesan and dot with a few flakes of butter. Brown in a pre-heated oven (180°C) for about 15 minutes, then serve.

BAKED LASAGNE

FOR THE PASTA: *(see basic recipe on page 138), 2 mozzarellas, grated Parmesan cheese, béchamel (see page 141), butter, salt.*
FOR THE SAUCE: *150 g minced beef, 50 g cooked ham in a single slice, 50 g sausage, 600 g tomato pulp, 1/2 onion, 1 small carrot, 1/2 celery stalk, 1 clove garlic, bay-leaf, basil, 1 clove, 1 piece cinnamon, 1/2 glass red wine, extra-virgin olive oil, salt, pepper.*

Prepare the pasta following the in-

structions given, boil, and lay to dry on a tea cloth.

Then prepare the sauce. Clean and chop the onion, carrot, celery and garlic, and chop the ham. Break up the sausage with a fork and sauté it lightly in a saucepan with a little oil, add the chopped vegetables and ham and mix well, leaving them to soften. Before the sauce begins to colour, add the minced beef and brown evenly, stirring all the time. Pour over the wine, let it evaporate, then add the tomato, the bay leaf, the spices and the salt. Lower the heat, cover, and leave to simmer slowly for about 1 hour. The sauce should be fairly liquid, since it is to be used poured over the layers of pasta.

While the meat sauce is cooking, prepare the béchamel.

Put a little meat sauce and a little béchamel in the bottom of a rectangular ovenproof dish, and blend them with a wooden spoon. Spread over this a first layer of lasagne, and sprinkle over diced mozzarella and grated Parmesan, cover with another layer of lasagne spread with meat sauce and béchamel. Continue, alternating the layers in this manner, until all the ingredients are used up, finishing with a layer of meat sauce and béchamel. Sprinkle with Parmesan, dot with a few flakes of butter, and cook in a pre-heated oven (200°C) for 30-40 minutes.

CANNELLONI WITH SAUSAGE AND MOZZARELLA

◆

FOR THE PASTA: (see basic recipe on page 137).
FOR THE SAUCE: 1 ladleful béchamel (see page 141), 4 dessertspoons tomato conserve, butter, grated Parmesan cheese.
FOR THE FILLING: 300 g spinach beet, 200 g sausage, 200 g mozzarella, 2 eggs, butter, grated Parmesan cheese, salt, pepper.

Wash and trim the spinach beet, scald in a little salted boiling water, squeeze, then chop finely. Skin the sausage and break up the meat with a fork, then put it in a saucepan and sauté it with the spinach beet in the butter. Cool, and tip into a bowl with the diced mozzarella, the eggs, a generous handful of grated Parmesan, a pinch of salt and one of pepper, then blend all the ingredients well together with a wooden spoon.

Cook the pasta, drain, and lay to dry on a tea cloth. Place the pasta squares on a floured work-surface, spread over the filling, and roll them up. Arrange the cannelloni in a buttered ovenproof dish, cover with béchamel, then spoon over the tomato conserve, sprinkle with grated Parmesan and dot with a few flakes of butter. Brown in a pre-heated oven (180°C) for about 15 minutes, then serve.

FANCY LASAGNE

◆

FOR THE PASTA: to basic recipe on page 138 add 300 g spinach, 20 g dried powdered tomatoes, 1 pinch dried red chilli.
FOR THE SAUCE: 200 g gorgonzola, 150 g pork sausage, 1 leek, 1 sprig rosemary, 40 g butter, 1 cup tomato sauce, 1 cup béchamel, grated Parmesan cheese, salt.

Divide the pasta dough into three parts. Proceed with the first in the normal manner; to the second add the spinach – boiled in a little salted water, squeezed, and processed in the blender; blend the dried tomato powder and a pinch of chilli powder well into the third part. Roll out the three types of pasta and cut into squares.

Chop the leek and the rosemary leaves, peel the sausage, break it up with a fork, and sauté all together in a saucepan with a little oil. Then add the tomato purée, and simmer for a while to reduce the water content. In another saucepan, melt the butter and the gorgonzola over a very low heat.

Cook the lasagne in plenty of salted water, then spread a layer in a buttered ovenproof dish. Cover with a little of the meat and tomato sauce, a layer of béchamel, and one of melted gorgonzola. Proceed with another layer of lasagne, alternating the colours, and garnish with the sauces in the same way. Continue until all the ingredients are used up, sprinkle the top layer generously with grated Parmesan and dot with a few flakes of butter. Brown in a pre-heated oven (180°C) for about half an hour, and serve.

Wash the chicken livers and chop them into pieces. Peel the sausage and mash up the meat with a fork, then add both, along with the minced veal and the bay leaves, to the sautéed mixture, seasoning with salt and pepper. Continue cooking over a medium heat, mixing well with a wooden spoon. Finally add the tomato sauce, and leave the sauce to simmer slowly until cooked.

Cook the lasagne and spread a first layer in a buttered ovenproof dish. Cover with a little of the sauce and some béchamel, sprinkle over a layer of grated Parmesan and one of grated Toma d'Alba cheese, and season with a little grated nutmeg. Continue building up the layers until all the ingredients are finished. Dot the top with a few flakes of butter, and brown in a pre-heated oven (200°C) for about 30-40 minutes. Serve piping hot.

91

LASAGNE, PIEDMONT STYLE

FOR THE PASTA: (see basic recipe on page 138).
FOR THE SAUCE: 100 g minced veal, 50 g sausage, 50 g chicken livers, 1 slice cooked salami, 1 small onion, 1 celery stalk, 1 sprig rosemary, 2 bay leaves, 1 cup tomato sauce, 1 cup béchamel, grated Parmesan cheese, mature Toma d'Alba cheese, extra-virgin olive oil, grated nutmeg, salt, pepper.

Chop up together the onion, celery, salami and rosemary leaves, then sauté them in a saucepan in the oil.

LASAGNE WITH HERBS

FOR THE PASTA: (see basic recipe on page 138).

FOR THE SAUCE: 200 g spinach, 200 g spinach beet, 100 g butter,

BAKED

1 clove garlic, 1 cup béchamel (*see page 141*), 1 sprig rosemary, grated Parmesan cheese, salt, pepper.

Wash and trim the vegetables. Cook them in a little boiling water, leave to cool, squeeze thoroughly and then chop finely. In a saucepan melt the butter, seasoning it with the garlic and rosemary. Cook the lasagne and spread a first layer in a buttered ovenproof dish. Cover with a layer of béchamel, then one of vegetable, sprinkle generously with grated Parmesan, moisten with the seasoned melted butter and flavour with a twist of freshly-ground pepper. Continue with similar layers, finishing with one of béchamel, grated Parmesan and butter. Brown in a pre-heated oven (200°C) for about 30-40 minutes, and serve piping hot.

LASAGNE WITH RICOTTA AND AUBERGINES

FOR THE PASTA: (*see basic recipe on page 138*).
FOR THE SAUCE: 300 g tomato pulp, 2 medium size aubergines, 180 g fresh ricotta cheese, 10 shelled walnuts, grated Parmesan cheese, extra-virgin olive oil, salt, pepper.

Prepare the basic pasta following the instructions in the recipe, then leave it to dry on a floured work-surface.
Set a saucepan on the heat and pour in a little oil and the sieved tomato pulp, season with salt and a pinch of pepper to prepare a sauce. In the meantime, blanch the walnuts then peel and crush them. Clean, wash and dry the aubergines, slice them and sprinkle with salt, and leave to rest for a couple of hours. Pour off the water, rinse and dry the aubergine slices, then deep-fry them in boiling oil. Lay on kitchen paper to absorb the excess oil, then chop. Set a large saucepan on the heat with plenty of water. When it boils, add salt and drop in the lasagne. Boil them a few at a time, and remove while they are still *al dente* with a slatted spoon. Then lay them on a tea cloth to dry. Spread a first layer of lasagne in an oiled ovenproof dish and cover it with the tomato sauce. Sprinkle over some chopped aubergines, a little crumbled ricotta, some of the crushed walnuts and grated Parmesan moistened with a little oil. Continue with similar layers, ending with one of lasagne covered with thinly sliced ricotta, a sprinkle of Parmesan and a trickle of oil. Cook in a pre-heated oven (180°C) for about ten minutes, and serve.

GREEN LASAGNE

FOR THE PASTA: to the basic recipe on page 138 add 300 g spinach.
FOR THE SAUCE: 150 g Castelmagro cheese, 150 g Dolcelatte cheese, 150 g fresh ricotta cheese, 40 g butter, grated Parmesan cheese, salt, grated nutmeg, pepper.

For the pasta, follow the instructions in

the basic recipe. Boil the spinach, drain, squeeze and process in the blender, then add to the pasta dough. Over a very low heat, melt in a saucepan the butter, Dolcelatte and Castelmagro. Boil the pasta, and spread a first layer in a buttered oven-proof dish. Cover with a layer of the melted cheese sauce, and then with one of ricotta, seasoning with a pinch of nutmeg and a grind of pepper. Continue layering the pasta and cheeses until all the ingredients are used up. Dot the top layer with a few flakes of butter, and sprinkle generously with grated Parmesan. Brown in a pre-heated oven (200°C) for 30-40 minutes, then serve.

MACCHERONI PASTICCIATI

◆

400 g maccheroni, 100 g Emmental, 100 g grated Parmesan cheese, 200 g fresh mushrooms, 1 clove garlic, 1 bunch parsley, béchamel (see page 141), extra-virgin olive oil, butter, salt, pepper.

Trim the mushrooms, removing the earthy residue with a damp cloth, slice them and stew lightly in a little oil flavoured with the crushed garlic. When they are cooked, remove the garlic and season with salt, pepper and chopped parsley.
Prepare the béchamel following the instructions, then stir in the diced Emmental and two dessertspoons of stewed mushrooms.
Boil the pasta in plenty of salted water,

drain it while it is still al dente, and mix in the mushrooms. In a buttered oven-proof dish arrange alternate layers of the pasta and mushroom mixture and the béchamel and grated Parmesan. Finish with a layer of béchamel and Parmesan and dot with a few flakes of butter. Cook in a pre-heated oven (180°C) for 15 minutes.

BAKED PIZZOCCHERI

300 g pizzoccheri (type of tagliatelle), 150 g grated Parmesan cheese, 150 g soft cheese (Fontina or Bitto), 200 g white cabbage or spinach beet, 200 g potatoes, 3 cloves garlic, 1 sprig sage, 100 g butter, extra-virgin olive oil, salt.

Wash the cabbage and potatoes, cut them into pieces and boil both in plenty of salted water. Put the pizzoccheri to boil in the same water, calculating the cooking-times so that all the ingredients can be drained al dente at the same time.
Meanwhile cut the soft cheese into thin slices, and melt the butter with a few spoonfuls of oil, flavouring with the sage and the crushed garlic cloves (removing the latter as soon as they begin to colour).
Spread a first layer of pasta and vegetable in an ovenproof dish, sprinkle with grated Parmesan and the slices of soft cheese, and season with the sage-flavoured butter. Continue building up similar layers, then complete with a gen-

erous sprinkle of Parmesan and dot with a few flakes of butter. Crisp in a pre-heated oven (200°C) for about 10 minutes.

der until all the ingredients are used up. Finish with a layer of tomato sauce, sprinkled with Parmesan and a few basil leaves. Cook in a pre-heated oven (180°C) for about 20 minutes before serving.

A richer version of this traditional Sicilian dish uses lard in the tomato sauce, while the aubergines are prepared dusted lightly with flour and fried in boiling oil.

MACCHERONI AND AUBERGINE PASTICCIO

◆

400 g maccheroni, 4 aubergines, 800 g tomato pulp, 1 onion, a few basil leaves, 2 Mozzarellas or 150 g Caciocavallo cheese, grated Parmesan cheese, extra-virgin olive oil, sugar, salt, chilli pepper.

Clean and slice the aubergines, sprinkle them with salt, and leave to drain for half an hour. Then rinse and dry them well and cook on a cast-iron griddle.

Prepare the sauce by sautéing the thinly sliced onion in a few spoonfuls of oil, and then adding the tomato. Stir in a pinch of sugar, salt and chilli pepper, and leave to simmer over a moderate heat for about 20 minutes, adding the basil just before you turn off the heat.

In the meantime, boil the pasta in plenty of salted water, drain it while it is still quite al dente, and dress with a trickle of oil. In a buttered ovenproof dish, start with a layer of tomato sauce, followed by one of sliced aubergines, one of sliced mozzarella, and one of pasta, completing with a sprinkle of Parmesan. Continue layering in this or-

FISH PASTICCIO

◆

FOR THE PASTA: (see basic recipe on page 138).
FOR THE SAUCE: 250 g squid, 200 g mussels, 200 g clams, 100 g scampi, 500 g peeled tomatoes, 3 cloves garlic, 1 bunch parsley, béchamel (see page 141), 1 glass dry white wine, extra-virgin olive oil, salt, 1 chilli pepper.

Prepare the pasta, boil in plenty of salted water and leave to dry on a tea cloth. Then prepare the sauce. Clean the different types of fish. Cut the squid in strips, and put the shellfish in a covered frying-pan over a rapid heat – as they open, remove the molluscs from the shells and when you have finished, sieve the cooking liquid and set aside.

In a saucepan gently heat a few spoonfuls of oil, flavouring with 2 cloves of garlic. As soon as it begins to colour, remove the garlic and add the squid; five minutes later add the rest of the fish. Pour over the wine and, as soon as this has evaporated, the shellfish cooking liquid. Then add the chopped peeled tomatoes and the crumbled chilli, and continue simmering for about 15-20 minutes. Chop the parsley and the remaining clove of garlic fine-

ly, add to the sauce and adjust salt to taste, then leave to cook for another few minutes before turning off the heat. Now prepare the béchamel. Spread a layer of fish sauce and béchamel in the bottom of an ovenproof dish and cover with a layer of pasta. Continue layering in this way until all the ingredients are used up. Finish with a layer of fish sauce, and sprinkle the surface with basil leaves. Brown in a pre-heated oven (200°C) for about half an hour, and serve.

OATFLAKE MOULD

300 g oatflakes, 50 g ricotta cheese, 3 eggs, 1 lemon, powdered cinnamon, red chilli pepper, 1/2 l milk, extra-virgin olive oil, salt.

Put the milk in a saucepan with 1/4 litre of water and bring to the boil. Then pour in the oatflakes, and stir until you have a fairly thick paste. Remove from the heat and leave to cool, then add the beaten egg yolks, the grated lemon peel, a pinch of salt, a pinch of cinnamon, a pinch of chilli pepper and a dessertspoon of oil. Blend all the ingredients well stirring with a wooden spoon, then gently fold in the stiffly-beaten egg whites. Finally pour into a lightly-oiled ovenproof dish, and cook in a moderate oven for about half an hour until a golden crust has formed. Re-

move from the oven, leave to cool for a while, then serve.

BAKED TAGLIATELLE WITH ASPARAGUS

400 g tagliatelle (see basic recipe on page 138), 1 kg asparagus, 250 g fresh ricotta cheese, 2 eggs, grated nutmeg, grated Parmesan cheese, extra-virgin olive oil, salt, pepper.

Clean the asparagus, cutting off the tougher parts of the stalks, and cook in boiling salted water for about 15 minutes. Drain and leave to drip slowly, then chop into pieces, discarding any parts which are still tough. Heat a little oil in a wide saucepan and sauté the asparagus until golden. Meanwhile, place the ricotta in a bowl and blend it with a little water, salt and pepper until you have a smooth cream. Heat a large saucepan full of water for the pasta, bring it to the boil, salt, and drop in the tagliatelle, draining them while they are still al dente. Stir olive oil and grated Parmesan into the pasta, then spread a first layer in an oiled ovenproof dish. Cover this with half the asparagus and half the ricotta cream, then proceed with another layer of tagliatelle, and one of asparagus and ricotta, finishing with a final layer of pasta. Beat the eggs, season with a little salt and pepper and a pinch of grated nutmeg, and stir in two dessertspoons of grated Parmesan. Pour this over the top of the pasta, and brown in a pre-heated oven (180°C) for about half an hour.

CAULIFLOWER
TIMBALLO

◆

400 g lasagne (see basic recipe on page 138), 1 large cauliflower, 1 clove garlic, 1 pinch grated nutmeg, powdered chilli pepper, béchamel (see page 141), 100 g grated Gruyère, 100 g grated Parmesan cheese, extra-virgin olive oil, salt.

Prepare the lasagne following the instructions given, boil in plenty of salted water, drain and leave to dry on a tea cloth. Wash the cauliflower, cut it into florets, and boil for a few minutes in a little water, drain. Sauté the cauliflower in a little oil in a frying-pan with the garlic, a pinch of chilli and one of grated nutmeg. Then prepare the béchamel, following the

instructions given and adding a handful of grated Parmesan and one of Gruyère. In an oiled ovenproof dish start with a layer of lasagne, followed by the béchamel, the grated Parmesan and Gruyère, and finally the cauliflower. Repeat the process until all the ingredients are used up, finishing with a layer of béchamel and the grated cheeses. Cook in a pre-heated oven (200°C) until a golden crust has formed on the top (about 15 minutes).

FENNEL
TIMBALLO

◆

400 g lasagne (see basic recipe on page 138), 1 kg fennel, 1 clove garlic, 1 pinch grated nutmeg, powdered chilli pepper, béchamel (see page 141), 100 g grated Gruyère, 100 g grated Parmesan cheese, extra-virgin olive oil, salt.

Prepare the lasagne following the instructions given, boil in plenty of salted water, drain and leave to dry on a tea cloth. Wash the fennel carefully, cut the heads vertically into wedges, and blanch in a little salted water. Drain while they are still *al dente*, and then sauté in a little oil in a frying-pan with the garlic, a pinch of chilli and one of grated nutmeg. Then prepare the béchamel, following the instructions given and adding a handful of grated Parmesan and one of Gruyère. In an oiled ovenproof dish start with a layer of lasagne, followed by the béchamel, the grated Parmesan and Gruyère, and finally the fennel. Repeat the process until all the ingredients are used up, finishing with a layer of béchamel and

the grated cheeses. Cook in a pre-heated oven (200°C) until the top is crispy and golden.

PEPPER TIMBALLO

◆

400 g lasagne (see basic recipe on page 138), 3 peppers, 2 ripe plum tomatoes, 1 onion, 1 large mozzarella, tomato sauce as required, powdered chilli pepper, grated Parmesan cheese, extra-virgin olive oil, salt.

Prepare the lasagne following the in-structions given, boil in plenty of salt-ed water, drain and leave to dry on a tea cloth. If you do not have any ready-made, prepare a good tomato sauce, starting with a sautéed base of finely-chopped carrot, celery and onion, and adding a little basil at the end of cooking. Then wash the peppers, remove the seeds and the white inner parts, and cut into strips. Place the peppers and the thinly sliced onion in a large frying-pan with a little oil, and sauté over a rapid heat for a few minutes, stirring with a wooden spoon, then lower the heat. When the peppers begin to soften, add two diced plum tomatoes, and season with salt and chilli pepper only towards the end of cooking. As soon as the peppers are ready, spread a layer of lasagne in an oiled ovenproof dish. Cover this with tomato sauce and then sprinkle with diced mozzarella, grated Parmesan and peppers. Repeat the layers until all the ingredients are used up, ending with a layer of lasagne, tomato sauce and grat-ed Parmesan. Cook in a pre-heated oven (200°C) for about twenty min-utes, then serve.

99

TIMBALLO CAPRICCIOSO

◆

400 g lasagne (see basic recipe on page 138), 800 g ripe firm tomatoes, 1 mozzarella, 2 aubergines, 2 pep-pers, 2 zucchini, 2 onions, 1 carrot, 1 celery stalk, oregano, powdered chilli pepper, grated Parmesan cheese, extra-virgin olive oil, salt.

Prepare the lasagne following the instructions given, boil in plenty of salted wa-ter, drain and leave to dry on a tea cloth. Wash, dry and cut into pieces the aubergines, zucchini and peppers (seeded and with the white inner parts removed). Place all the vegetables in a frying-pan with the thinly-sliced onion and a little oil, and sauté for a few minutes over a moderate heat. Then lower the heat and leave to simmer, adding a little salt and a pinch of chilli just before removing from the heat.

Meanwhile prepare a tomato sauce. Plunge the tomatoes in boiling water for a few minutes, then peel, seed and chop them, finely chop the onion, celery and carrot, and cook all together with a pinch of oregano. When the sauce is nearly cooked, tip it in with the other vegetables and leave on the heat for a few minutes to allow the flavours to blend.

Spread a layer of lasagne in an oiled ovenproof dish, and cover with the tomato and vegetable sauce, then sprinkle with diced mozzarella and grated Parmesan. Repeat the layers until all the ingredients are used up, finishing with a layer of lasagne, tomato and Parmesan. Cook in a pre-heated oven (200°C) for about twenty minutes.

VEGETARIAN TIMBALLO

◆

400 g spaghetti, 300 g freshly shelled peas, 3 artichokes, 1/2 onion, red chilli pepper, 100 g Gruyère, breadcrumbs, extra-virgin olive oil, salt.

Remove the tougher outer leaves from the artichokes, cut off the tips, cut them into thin wedges and dip in water mixed with a little lemon juice.

Slice the onion thinly and sauté in a frying-pan in a little oil. After a few minutes, add the peas and the artichokes, season with salt and chilli pepper, cover, and leave to simmer on a moderate heat.

When the vegetables are almost cooked, bring a large saucepan of water to the boil, salt, and tip in the spaghetti. Drain while they are still *al dente*, and season with a trickle of oil. In an oiled ovenproof dish spread a layer of spaghetti and cover with the thinly-sliced Gruyère. Then spread the vegetables in the middle, and cover with another layer of spaghetti. Sprinkle the top with breadcrumbs, and cook in a pre-heated oven (180°C) for about twenty minutes. Turn out onto a serving-dish and serve hot.

all the ingredients are used up, finishing with a layer of spinach and Parmesan. Cook in a pre-heated moderate oven until the top is golden (about half an hour).

SPINACH
TIMBALLO

◆

400 g lasagne (*see basic recipe on page 138*), 1 kg spinach, 400 g ricotta cheese, 1 pinch grated nutmeg, powdered chilli pepper, 100 g grated Parmesan cheese, extra-virgin olive oil, salt.

Prepare the lasagne following the instructions given; boil in plenty of salted water, drain and leave to dry on a tea cloth.
Trim the spinach, wash carefully, and cook in a little lightly salted water. Drain and squeeze well, then chop finely and mix with the mashed ricotta, adding a little of the spinach cooking water or milk, if necessary, until the mixture has a smooth, creamy consistency. Complete by stirring in the grated Parmesan, a pinch of salt, one of chilli pepper and one of grated nutmeg.
Spread a layer of lasagne in an oiled ovenproof dish, then cover with a layer of spinach and ricotta and sprinkle with grated Parmesan. Repeat the layers in the same way until

BUCATINI
PIE

◆

200 g bucatini, 400 g potatoes, 200 g peeled tomatoes, 2 onions, oregano, basil, 50 g grated Parmesan cheese, 3 dessertspoons extra-virgin olive oil, salt, pepper.

Peel and slice the potatoes, and spread a layer in the bottom of a high-sided cake-tin. Sieve the tomatoes, or pass them through a food-mill, and pour a little of the purée over the potatoes. Slice one of the onions very finely and scatter over the potato and tomato. Pour over two dessertspoons of oil and a little grated Parmesan, salt, pepper and sprinkle generously with oregano and basil. Over this spread a layer of bucatini broken into pieces.
Repeat the layers of potato, tomatoes, onion and bucatini, seasoning as before, and finishing with a layer of potatoes, since the pasta must be buried in the centre of the pie.
Pour over enough water to cover the pasta layers, and cook over a low heat for about 20 minutes. Stir every so often with a wooden spoon, being careful not to mix up the layers of the pie; when cooked the dish should emerge almost as if it had been steamed.

VINCISGRASSI

◆

FOR THE PASTA: 400 g flour, 200 g semolina, 5 eggs, 40 g butter, Vin santo (sweet wine), salt.
FOR THE BÉCHAMEL: see page 141.
FOR THE SAUCE: 100 g bacon fat, 1 onion, 300 g chicken giblets, 450 g veal sweetbreads-bone marrow, 250 g tomato pulp, grated nutmeg, white wine, stock as required, 200 g grated Parmesan cheese, butter, extra-virgin olive oil, salt, pepper.

Put the flour, the semolina, the eggs, the melted butter, a little salt and a finger of Vin santo into a bowl, and mix thoroughly. Knead well and then leave to rest for about half an hour. Roll the pastry out thin and cut into strips about 10 - 15 cm long. Boil it in plenty of salted water, and when it is half-cooked, drain, and leave to dry on tea cloths.
Prepare the sauce: chop the bacon fat and the onion and sauté them in the oil in a saucepan, then add the finely chopped chicken giblets, leave to brown for a few minutes, stirring, and then pour over the white wine. As soon as this has evaporated, add the tomato pulp and season with salt, pepper and a pinch of grated nutmeg. After about a quarter of an hour add the chopped sweet-breads and bone marrow, salt, cover and leave to simmer for about an hour and a half – adding hot stock if necessary.
In the meantime prepare the béchamel following the instructions given.
Butter an ovenproof dish and spread layers of pasta, a little béchamel, grated Parmesan, sauce, and a few knobs of butter. Repeat the layers until all the ingredients are used up, finishing with a layer of pasta covered with béchamel and grated Parmesan. Cook in a pre-heated oven at 200°C for about 30-40 minutes. Serve piping hot.

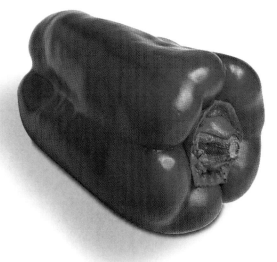

GNOCCHI
AND FILLED PASTA

AGNOLOTTI WITH BASS

◆

FOR THE PASTA: *see basic recipe on page 138.*
FOR THE FILLING: *250 g bass, 50 g ricotta cheese, 1 egg, 1 dessertspoon grated Parmesan cheese, 1 sprig basil, grated nutmeg, butter, salt.*
FOR THE SAUCE: *8 artichoke hearts, 2 sage leaves, 50 g butter.*

Lightly brown the bass meat in a little butter, then remove the bones and the skin and mash it with a fork. Beat the egg in a bowl, season with a pinch of salt and one of grated nutmeg, then add the ricotta, the fish, a dessertspoon of grated Parmesan and the chopped basil and blend all the ingredients thoroughly. Roll out the pasta, made following the base recipe provided, and arrange the filling in small mounds at regular intervals. Cover with a second layer of pasta, then press down with your fingertips around each filled section to eliminate air-pockets. Cut out 3cm squares with a pastry wheel.
Cut the artichoke hearts into small wedges, dip them in water mixed with a little lemon juice, then drain and sauté lightly in a little butter.
Melt the rest of the butter in an-other saucepan, flavouring it with the sage. Cook the agnolotti in plenty of salted water, drain and tip into a large serving bowl. Stir in the artichoke hearts, pour over the melted butter, and serve immediately.

AGNOLOTTI NEAPOLITAN STYLE

FOR THE PASTA: *see basic recipe on page 138*
FOR THE FILLING: *300 g ricotta cheese, 2 eggs, 1 large mozzarella, 1 handful basil leaves, salt, pepper.*
FOR THE SAUCE: *500 g tomato pulp, 1 onion, a few basil leaves, 300 g beef, red wine, extra-virgin olive oil, salt, pepper.*

Start by preparing the pasta for the agnolotti following the instructions given. Then prepare the filling by blending the ricotta in a bowl with the 2 eggs, the basil, the chopped mozzarella, a pinch of salt and a twist of freshly-ground pepper.
To prepare the sauce, soften the chopped onion in an earthenware pot in a few spoonfuls of oil, then add the meat cut into pieces and sauté, stirring all the time. Season with salt, sprinkle over a little red wine, and after a few minutes add the tomato pulp. Cook over a low heat for about an hour, and before switching off the heat add the basil leaves torn into pieces and pepper.
Roll out the pasta on a floured work-surface, and cut it into large circles. Place a little of the filling in the centre of each disk, then fold up the pasta to

form the agnolotti, pressing the edges tightly together to remove any air from inside.

Boil the agnolotti in plenty of salted water, drain and serve with the meat sauce and, if desired, with a sprinkle of Parmesan cheese.

AGNOLOTTI WITH TRUFFLE

◆

<u>FOR THE PASTA:</u> *see basic recipe on page 138.*
<u>FOR THE FILLING:</u> 150 g lean pork, 150 g Parma ham, 100 g veal, 1/2 black or white truffle, 1 egg, dry white wine (optional), grated Parmesan cheese, 50 g butter, salt, pepper.
<u>FOR THE SAUCE:</u> 1/2 truffle, grated Parmesan cheese, butter.

Prepare the pasta for the agnolotti following the instructions given.

Place in a saucepan the butter, the minced veal and pork, the chopped ham, half the truffle – cleaned and sliced thinly using a special truffle-slicer – the egg, a handful of grated Parmesan, salt and pepper. Cook over a low heat, stirring well and moistening with a little white wine only if necessary. When it is all thoroughly cooked, roll out the pasta into a large sheet and arrange small heaps of the filling at regular intervals over half of it. Fold over the other half, press down, and cut into the desired shapes with a pastry wheel. Leave the agnolotti to air on a tea cloth for about half an hour.

Bring a large saucepan of salted water to the boil, then drop in the agnolotti, removing them with a slatted spoon as soon as they come to the surface. Lay them on a hot serving-dish and sprinkle them with grated Parmesan and melted butter, and complete the dish by grating over them the half of the truffle not used in the filling.

POTATO AGNOLOTTI

◆

<u>FOR THE PASTA:</u> *see basic recipe on page 138.*
<u>FOR THE FILLING:</u> 600 g potatoes, 1 onion, 3 leaves mint, 1 pinch cinnamon, 1 measure cognac, butter, salt, pepper.
<u>FOR THE SAUCE:</u> grated smoked ricotta cheese, butter.

Prepare the pasta for the agnolotti following the instructions given. Boil, peel and mash the potatoes, then stir in the salt and pepper, the cognac, the chopped mint and a pinch of cinnamon. Mix the ingredients well, then slice the onion finely, sauté lightly in a little butter and blend into the potato mixture.

Roll out the pasta into a large sheet. Place piles of the filling at regular intervals over half of it, then fold over, and press down with your fingertips around each filled section. Cut out the agnolotti with a pastry wheel.

Bring a large pan of water to the boil, salt lightly and drop in the agnolotti. Drain and serve with the melted butter poured over, and sprinkled with the grated smoked ricotta.

SPINACH DUMPLINGS

◆

300 g stale bread, 800 g spinach, 1 glass milk, 2 eggs, 1 small onion, 1 clove garlic, 1 dessertspoon wheatmeal flour, 4 dessertspoons grated Parmesan cheese, 2 dessertspoons breadcrumbs, 1 pinch grated nutmeg, 100 g butter, salt, pepper.

Among the many different recipes for dumplings we have selected this one, since it is the most suitable for serving without broth. Start by dicing the stale bread and steeping it in warm milk. Then trim and wash the spinach, and boil it a little salted water or steam it. Chop the garlic and onion and sauté in a large saucepan in a little butter, then add the drained and squeezed spinach, and continue to sauté over a moderate heat. In a large bowl, mix the beaten eggs with the bread, add the spinach and blend thoroughly, seasoning with salt, a pinch of pepper and the grated nutmeg, then stir in the flour and the breadcrumbs. Shape the mixture into small dumplings, then drop them into a large pan of boiling salted water and cook for 15 minutes with the water boiling gently. Remove with a slatted spoon, and serve with the melted butter poured over and sprinkled with grated Parmesan.

CASONCELLI

◆

<u>FOR THE PASTA:</u> *500 g white flour, 1 pinch salt, 5 eggs.*
<u>FOR THE FILLING:</u> *300 g beef, 1 carrot, 1 small celery stalk, 1/2 onion, 1 clove, 1 pinch grated nutmeg, 3-4 basil leaves, 1 egg yolk, 1/2 glass full-bodied red wine, 50 g grated Parmesan cheese, 50 g fine breadcrumbs, butter, 2 dessert-spoons extra-virgin olive oil, salt, pepper.*
<u>FOR THE SAUCE:</u> *a few sage leaves, 100 g grated Grana cheese, 120 g butter.*

On a floured board, mix the flour with a pinch of salt, four whole eggs and one yolk, adding a little water if necessary. Knead well for about ten minutes, then roll out two thin sheets, being careful not to let them dry out.
In a saucepan sauté the thinly sliced onion in a generous knob of butter and the olive oil, put in the beef and brown it on all sides, then sprinkle over the wine and let it evaporate. Clean and chop the carrot and celery and tip them into the meat saucepan along with the clove, the chopped basil, salt, pepper and a pinch of grated nutmeg. Cover, and leave to simmer for two and a half hours, adding a little hot water from time to time if necessary.
When it is cooked, chop the meat up small and pass the vegetables through a food-mill. Tip both into a bowl, and add the breadcrumbs, the grated Grana and the egg yolk. Blend all the ingredients thoroughly, and adjust salt to taste.
Lay this mixture in small heaps at regular intervals on one sheet of the pasta. Lay the second sheet over the first and press down with your fingertips around each filled section to seal thoroughly. Use a pastry wheel to divide into squares of about 4cm, then leave to dry on a lightly-floured tea-cloth.
Cook the casoncelli in plenty of boil-

ing salted water for about 10 minutes, drain thoroughly, and tip into a hot serving-dish, pour over the melted butter flavoured with sage, and sprinkle with grated Grana. Allow the flavours to blend for a few seconds before serving.

CREPES GRATIN

◆

FOR THE CREPES: 250 g milk, 125 g flour, 2 eggs, 30 g butter, salt.

The presentation of a plate of crepes at the table is always greatly appreciated by the assembled diners. They lend a touch of class to the simplest meals, and, contrary to popular belief, can be very easily prepared with a minimum of organisation.

108

The range of possible fillings is endless, these can be prepared with vegetables, cheese, meat or fish. Here we limit ourselves to the more traditional recipes, the creation of more imaginative combinations being left to the imaginative flair of

each individual cook. All involve the preparation of the basic crepe batter and of a béchamel sauce, which is useful both for binding the filling and for pouring over the finished dish.

The quantities given are sufficient for about 12 crepes. Beat the eggs, flour and a pinch of salt with an egg-whisk, then, continuing to whisk, dilute with the milk, and the butter previously melted over a low heat.

Lightly oil and heat an 18cm diameter non-stick frying-pan, then pour on a ladleful of batter. When the crepe is golden on one side, flip it over with a fish slice and brown the other. Continue until all the batter is used up.

If you wish, you can prepare the crepes the day before and store them in the fridge covered with clingfilm.

WITH RED CHICORY FILLING

600 g red chicory, 1 onion, béchamel (see page 141), grated Parmesan cheese, dry white wine, salt, pepper.

Wash and slice the onion and the chicory, then sauté lightly in a saucepan with a little oil. Sprinkle the vegetables with white wine, season with salt and pepper, lower the heat and continue cooking for another ten minutes.

Prepare the béchamel and mix half of it with the chicory. Use this to fill the crepes, then fold them in four, and arrange slightly overlapping in a buttered ovenproof dish. Pour over the rest of the béchamel, sprinkle with grated

Parmesan, and dot with a few flakes of butter. Brown in a hot oven at 180°C.

WITH SHELLFISH
FILLING

◆

500 g prawns and scampi, 1 small lobster, 2 cloves garlic, 1 bunch parsley, 1/2 dose béchamel, (see recipe page 141), cooking cream, 1/2 measure brandy, extra-virgin olive oil, butter, salt, pepper.

Wash the prawns and scampi, remove the shells, and sauté for about 5-6 minutes in a frying-pan with a knob of butter. Prepare a shellfish fumet with the shells and the lobster (see page 114). When cooked, drain the lobster and remove the flesh, then sieve the cooking juices and set aside.

In a saucepan sauté the garlic cloves in a few dessertspoons of oil; as soon as they begin to brown, remove them and add the finely chopped shellfish meat. Stir gently, letting the flavours blend, then pour over the brandy and when it has almost all evaporated, add a few spoonfuls of the fish juices (fumet) thickened with a little flour. Leave the sauce to reduce, and adjust salt and pepper to taste before switching off the heat.

Prepare the béchamel (you can even use the lobster fumet instead of the milk) and as soon as it begins to boil, add a little chopped parsley and dilute with the cream. Continue cooking, stirring all the time, until the sauce has the right consistency (which should be rather more liquid than a normal béchamel).

Place a spoonful of the fish sauce in the centre of each crepe, fold in four,

and then arrange them slightly overlapping in a buttered ovenproof dish. Pour over the béchamel and dot with a few flakes of butter. Brown in a hot oven (200°C) for about ten minutes before serving.

POTATO CULINGIONIS

FOR THE PASTA: 500 g white flour, water.
FOR THE FILLING: 600 g potatoes, 1 onion, 2 cloves garlic, fresh mint, 300 g grated mature Pecorino cheese, extra-virgin olive oil, salt.
FOR THE SAUCE: butter, or tomato sauce (see page 143).

In a bowl or on a floured work-surface, mix the flour with enough warm water to produce a smooth elastic dough. Add a little salt and knead thoroughly, then form into a ball, cover with a clean tea-cloth and leave to rise.

In the meantime peel, wash and boil the potatoes, then mash them in a bowl together with the grated Pecorino and a pinch of salt. Peel and chop the onion and garlic and a few mint leaves, and sauté in a little oil for a few minutes (preferably in an earthenware pot), then add to the potato mixture. When it is thoroughly blended, roll the mixture into small balls.

Roll out the pasta into two thin sheets, and arrange the potato balls at regular intervals over one half. Place the other sheet of pasta on top, press down with your fingertips in the spaces between the filled sections, and cut out with a pastry wheel, sealing the edges well.

Boil in plenty of salted water, then drain and pour over the melted butter

or the tomato sauce. Before serving, sprinkle generously with grated Pecorino.

FLORENTINE GNOCCHI

◆

1 kg potatoes, 300 g spinach, 200 g white flour, 1 egg, a few sage leaves, butter, grated Parmesan cheese, salt.

Peel the potatoes and boil them in salted water. Cook the spinach in a little boiling water, then squeeze thoroughly. Mash the potatoes and sieve the spinach, then bind them together with the help of the beaten egg. Stir in the flour, adding a little more if the mixture still seems too soft. Roll out into long sausages and cut them into lengths of about 2 cm, then lay on a floured tea cloth. Bring a large saucepan of salted water to the boil and drop in the gnocchi, removing them with a slatted spoon as soon as they come to the surface. Melt the butter, flavouring it with the sage, and pour over the gnocchi on a serving-dish, then sprinkle generously with grated Parmesan.

SPINACH GNOCCHI

◆

1 kg spinach, 350 g ricotta cheese, 2 egg yolks, grated Parmesan cheese, flour, a few sage leaves, butter, grated nutmeg, salt, pepper.

Clean the spinach carefully and boil in a little salted water, drain and squeeze thoroughly, then chop finely. In a bowl, mash the ricotta with a fork then add the spinach and bind together with the egg yolks and 2 dessertspoons of Parmesan, seasoning with salt, pepper and grated nutmeg. With the help of a teaspoon shape the mixture into balls about the size of a walnut and roll them in flour, then tip into a large saucepan of boiling salted water.

Remove them carefully with a slatted spoon as soon as they come to the surface. Serve with melted butter flavoured with sage, and sprinkled with grated Parmesan.

VALLE D'AOSTA GNOCCHI

◆

200 g coarse corn meal, 100 g fine corn meal, 150 g Fontina cheese, 2 egg yolks, grated nutmeg, 1 l milk, grated Parmesan cheese, butter, salt, pepper.

Pour the milk into a saucepan and heat. When it is about to boil, tip in the two types of corn meal and a pinch of salt, beating with an egg-whisk. Continue cooking like a normal polenta, stirring occasionally. When it is cooked, after about 40 minutes, stir in the diced Fontina, a dessertspoon of butter and a pinch of grated nutmeg. Leave to cool slightly, then blend in the two egg yolks and roll out about 1 cm thick on a floured surface. When it has cooled, use a glass to cut out disks of about 4 or 5 cm, then lay them overlapping in a buttered ovenproof dish. Sprinkle with grated Parmesan and pepper, pour over the melted butter and brown in a hot oven for about ten minutes before serving.

The unique feature of this traditional Trieste dish is that it can be served as a first course, garnished with breadcrumbs lightly fried in butter, as a second course to accompany game, and also as a sweet course, with melted butter poured over and sprinkled with sugar and cinnamon to taste.

PRUNE GNOCCHI

◆

1 kg potatoes, 1 kg dried prunes, 200 g white flour, 1 egg, 30 g butter, sugar as required, salt.

With the above ingredients (excepting of course the prunes and the sugar) prepare a mixture as for normal potato gnocchi, but then make it up into large gnocchi about twice the usual size. Make a hollow in each one with your fingers, and insert a prune with the stone removed and replaced with a teaspoon of sugar. A useful guide is to have about as much potato as prune in each of the gnocchi. Bring a large saucepan of salted water to the boil and drop in the gnocchi. From the moment they come to the surface, calculate about 15 minutes cooking time.

POTATO GNOCCHI WITH TOMATO

◆

1 kg potatoes, 200 g white flour, 500 g tomato pulp, 1 onion, a few sage leaves, butter, salt, pepper.

Boil the potatoes in their skins, then peel and mash them while they are still hot. Tip them onto a floured work-surface, and lightly incorporate the salt and enough flour to produce the right consistency. (The gnocchi will be soft if they are made using only a little flour and, ideally, floury "gnocchi potatoes"). Roll the mixture into finger size sausages, then cut into pieces, and give them the typical gnocchi shape by pushing over the back of a grater.

Prepare the sauce: put the tomato pulp and the onion cut into wedges into a large saucepan with a knob of butter, salt and pepper. Cook over a moderate heat for about 15 minutes, then switch off and remove the onion. In another small saucepan, brown a good wedge of butter, flavouring it with a few sage leaves.

113

SHELLFISH FUMET

250 g fish leftovers or mixed second-rate fish, 1 onion, 1 carrot, 1 celery stalk, bay leaves, sage, thyme, juniper berries, 1 large slice of lemon, a little white wine, salt, peppercorns.

Put the fish in a large saucepan with 2 litres of water, the onion cut into wedges, the roughly chopped celery and carrot, the herbs, a handful of salt, a few peppercorns, the lemon and the wine. Bring to the boil on a moderate heat, skimming frequently, and then simmer for about 40 minutes. Sieve the fish stock thoroughly before use. It can also be enriched by adding the puréed fish meat.

Bring a large saucepan of salted water to the boil and drop in the gnocchi a few at a time. As soon as they rise to the surface, remove with a slatted spoon and serve directly on the dinner plates, spooning over the tomato sauce and a little melted butter. Offer the grated Parmesan separately.

Gnocchi constitute an excellent first course, and can be served with various sauces: tomato, meat sauce, pesto or a sauce made with four different types of cheese.

FISH GNOCCHI

◆

600 g potatoes, 300 g sole fillets (or other delicate fish), 2 anchovy fillets in oil, 400 g tomato pulp, 1 bunch herbs (sage, rosemary, marjoram), 1 shallot, 1 onion, 1 clove garlic, 1 dessertspoon olive paste, 1 egg, about 150 g white flour, dry white wine, extra-virgin olive oil, salt, pepper.

Chop the garlic and onion very finely and sauté in two dessertspoons of oil, then add the fish cut into pieces and let the flavours blend for a few min-

utes. Pour over the white wine and – when it has almost completely evaporated – season with salt and pepper and leave on the heat for a few more minutes. Leave to cool then whiz in the blender.

Boil the potatoes in salted water. Peel them while they are still hot, mash, and tip them onto a floured worksurface. Make a well in the centre, break in the egg and add the fish. Blend all the ingredients thoroughly, adding the flour gradually, and knead into a smooth paste of the right consistency.

Keeping the gnocchi mixture warm, prepare the sauce. In a saucepan sauté the finely chopped shallot in a little oil, then stir in the anchovies until they disintegrate. Add the olive paste, the chopped tomato pulp, salt and pepper, and cook for five minutes, stirring in the chopped herbs just before you switch off the heat.

Roll the gnocchi paste into long sausages and chop into short lengths, use the prongs of a fork to give them the typical gnocchi shape, or rub them over the back of a grater. Bring a large saucepan of salted water to the boil and drop in the gnocchi a few at a time. Remove with a slatted spoon as soon as they come to the surface, and serve with the tomato and anchovy sauce.

RICOTTA GNOCCHI

◆

400 g fresh ricotta cheese, 300 g white flour, breadcrumbs, 2 eggs, grated Parmesan cheese, a few sage leaves, extra-virgin olive oil, butter, ginger, nutmeg, salt.

Put the ricotta in a bowl and beat vigorously with a wooden spoon until it is creamy. Add 3 or 4 dessertspoons of oil, the eggs, a pinch of salt, 3 dessertspoons of grated Parmesan, a pinch of freshly grated ginger and one of nutmeg. Finally stir in the flour, and enough breadcrumbs to stiffen the mixture sufficiently. Blend thoroughly, then put in the fridge for half an hour. When the time is up, roll into long sausages and chop them into gnocchi of the desired length.
Boil in plenty of salted water and drain, a few at a time, on a slatted spoon. Serve the gnocchi with the melted butter flavoured with sage poured over them, and sprinkled generously with grated Parmesan.

SEMOLINA GNOCCHI

◆

250 g semolina, 1 l milk, 2 egg yolks, 150 g butter, 100 g Parmesan cheese, a few sage leaves, grated nutmeg, salt.

Pour the milk and half a litre of water into a large saucepan with a pinch of salt. Heat, and when it begins to boil, sprinkle over the semolina, beating all the time so that it does not become lumpy. After about ten minutes, switch off the heat and leave to cool slightly. Then stir in the egg yolks, a pinch of nutmeg and a little Parmesan, blending thoroughly. Pour out onto a (preferably marble) work-surface, spread out about 1 cm thick using a spatula, then leave to cool. Using a special cutter, or a glass with a moistened rim, cut into circles (or if you prefer, simply cut into lozenges) and arrange slightly overlapping in a buttered ovenproof dish. Sprinkle generously with grated Parmesan and a few chopped sage leaves, dot with flakes of butter and brown in a hot oven (200°C) for about 15 minutes.

115

PUMPKIN GNOCCHI

◆

1 1/2 kg sweet yellow pumpkin, 250 g white flour, 2 eggs, 150 g grated Parmesan cheese, 100 g butter, ginger, salt, chilli pepper.

Peel the pumpkin and remove the seeds, then boil it in water or steam it.

Once cooked, drain and mash, and put it into a bowl with the flour, the eggs, a pinch of salt, a pinch of chilli pepper and one of freshly grated ginger. Blend all the ingredients thoroughly into a paste, then roll out into long sausages and chop up into gnocchi-length pieces. Drop a few at a time into a large saucepan of lightly salted water, removing them with a slotted spoon as soon as they come to the surface. Tip into a serving-dish, pour over the melted butter and sprinkle with grated Parmesan.

116

GNOCCHI
GRATIN
◆

1 kg potatoes, 3 eggs, 1 cup béchamel (see page 141), 4 dessertspoons of cooking cream, grated Parmesan cheese, 80 g butter, salt.

Choose suitable floury potatoes. Boil them, then peel and mash while they are still hot. Stir in the salt, 2 eggs, 50 g butter and 3 dessertspoons of grated Parmesan, blending thoroughly. Spread out the mixture on a buttered work-surface, levelling it out about 1 cm thick, and leave to cool. Then cut out disks using a special cutter or a glass with a moistened rim.
Prepare the béchamel following the instructions given. Butter an ovenproof dish and arrange the gnocchi in layers, covering each with béchamel and grated Parmesan. Brown in a hot oven for about ten minutes.

LANGAROLI

<u>FOR THE PASTA</u>: *(see basic recipe on page 138).*
<u>FOR THE FILLING</u>: *100 g boiled beef, 50 g boiled rice, 50 g white cabbage, 50 g grated mature Toma d'Alba cheese, 2 eggs, grated nutmeg, butter, salt, pepper.*
<u>FOR THE SAUCE</u>: *150 g minced leg of veal, 2 ripe firm tomatoes, 1 leek, 1 sprig rosemary, grated Parmesan cheese, extra-virgin olive oil, salt, pepper.*

Wash and dry the cabbage leaves, cut into thin strips and sauté them lightly in a saucepan in the butter. Add the minced boiled beef, season with salt, pepper and nutmeg and brown, stirring, for a few minutes. Remove from the heat and let the meat cool before adding the eggs the boiled rice and the grated Toma d'Alba. Blend all the ingredients thoroughly. Roll out the pasta into two thin sheets, and lay teaspoonfuls of the filling at regular intervals on one. Cover with the second sheet of pasta, then press down with your fingertips around each filled section. With a knife cut the pasta into squares of about 1 1/2 cm, then seal the edges by pinching them all round between thumb and forefinger.
Put the finely chopped leek into a saucepan with the rosemary and sauté lightly in the oil, add the minced veal and brown for a few minutes, stirring all the time. Plunge the tomatoes into boiling water for a few minutes, peel, seed and chop them and tip them into the saucepan. Season with salt and pepper, and leave to reduce over a moderate heat.
Bring a large pan of salted water to the boil and cook the langaroli. Drain and tip into a warm serving-dish, pour over

the meat sauce and sprinkle with grated Parmesan before serving.

RAVIOLI

◆

FOR THE PASTA: (*see basic recipe on page 138*).

Ravioli come in a wide variety of shapes and fillings. Different shapes of ravioli can be created by using the different pasta cutters which are available. As for the filling, you can either use the classic meat or ricotta stuffings (recommended for tortellini and tortelloni) or one of the three fillings suggested below.
The first step involves the preparation of the pasta following the basic recipe provided.
When you have prepared the selected filling, roll out the pasta thinly on a floured work-surface, and arrange small piles of the filling at regular intervals. Fold over the other half of the sheet of pasta, and use the special cutters to cut the ravioli into the desired shape. A useful tip is to brush the pasta between the filled sections with beaten egg white, this helps to bind the two layers when the edges of the ravioli are pressed together.
Leave the prepared ravioli in a cool place for about a day, then cook them in plenty of salted water. Drain, and serve with melted butter and grated Parmesan, or with a light tomato sauce, as desired.

MUSHROOM FILLING

◆

250 g fresh ricotta cheese, 250 g fresh mushrooms, grated Parmesan cheese, 1 clove garlic, 1 bunch parsley, extra-virgin olive oil, salt, pepper.

Clean the mushrooms, removing the clay with a damp cloth, then slice them and stew in a saucepan with a little oil and the crushed garlic clove. Before switching off the heat, season with salt, pepper and finely-chopped parsley. Remove the garlic, and chop the mushrooms very fine. In a bowl, mash the ricotta thoroughly with a fork, beating until it is creamy, add a little grated Parmesan, then stir in the mushroom mixture.

FISH FILLING

◆

400 g boiled fish, 2 eggs, a few sage leaves, 1 dessertspoon chopped pistachios, 120 g grated Parmesan cheese, butter or extra-virgin olive oil, grated nutmeg, salt.

Remove the skin and bones from the fish, chop it up, then put it into a bowl with the grated Parmesan, the eggs, salt, and a pinch of nutmeg, and blend the ingredients thoroughly.
Different types of fish may be used (trout, sturgeon etc.) providing a varied range of flavours. Accompany the ravioli with cream and a little tomato sauce.

ARTICHOKE FILLING

◆

5 artichokes, 1/2 onion, 1/2 clove garlic, 1 bunch parsley, 1 lemon, 80 g ricotta cheese, 3 dessertspoons of grated Parmesan cheese, 2 eggs, salt.

Clean the artichokes, removing most of the stalk, the tips and the tough outer leaves. Cut into wedges and steep in water mixed with lemon juice for half an hour.
Chop the garlic and onion, and sauté

them till soft in a saucepan in a little oil. Add the thinly-sliced artichokes, and continue cooking over a moderate heat for about 30-40 minutes, adding a little hot water every so often. Before switching off the heat, season with salt, pepper and chopped parsley. Leave to cool. In a bowl, blend the ricotta with the eggs, the grated Parmesan and a pinch of salt, then stir in the finely chopped artichokes and mix thoroughly.

REDFISH RAVIOLI

◆

FOR THE PASTA: (see basic recipe on page 138).
FOR THE FILLING: 400 g cleaned redfish meat, 1 bunch mixed herbs, 1 egg yolk, 1 clove garlic, 1 lemon, 1 dessertspoon mascarpone cheese, extra-virgin olive oil, salt, pepper.
FOR THE SAUCE: butter, chives.

In a saucepan, sauté the crushed garlic clove in plenty of oil. As soon as it is golden, remove it and tip in the fish, seasoning with a pinch of salt and a little grated lemon zest. Let the flavours merge for a few minutes, then switch off the heat.
Chop the redfish meat and blend it carefully with the mascarpone, the finely-chopped mixed herbs, the egg yolk, salt and pepper.
Prepare the ravioli using the recommended dough. Roll out a thin layer of pasta, then cut out squares of 5x5 cm with the special cutter or a pastry wheel. Place a teaspoon of the filling in the centre of each one, then place an-

other square on top, and form into the typical ravioli shape.
Boil the ravioli in plenty of salted water or stock (vegetable or fish), draining them while they are still al dente. Before serving, mix with the melted butter and sprinkle with chopped chives.

119

SOLE RAVIOLI

◆

FOR THE PASTA: (see basic recipe on page 138)
FOR THE FILLING: 200 g sole fillets, 150 g borage, 50 g ricotta cheese, 2 eggs, grated Parmesan cheese, salt, pepper.
FOR THE SAUCE: 150 g shelled clams, 1 clove garlic, 1 bunch parsley, 1 cup tomato sauce.

Blanch the borage in salted boiling water, drain, squeeze and chop. Sauté the sole in the butter then mash it with a fork. Tip the fish and the borage into a bowl, add the eggs, the ricotta, a pinch of salt, one of pepper and a handful of grated Parmesan cheese, then mix all well together with a wooden spoon. Roll out the pasta into a thin sheet, arrange small heaps of the mixture at regular intervals over half of it, then fold over the pasta, and press down well with your fingertips around the filled sections. Using a pastry wheel, cut out the pasta into squares of about 2.5 cm.

Steep the clams in salted water for at least half an hour, then open them in a covered frying pan over a very lively heat. Remove the shells, then sieve the juices and set aside. Chop the garlic and parsley finely and sauté lightly in oil, add the clams, the tomato sauce and the sieved cooking juices and leave to reduce. Cook the ravioli in plenty of boiling salted water, drain and tip into a serving-bowl. Pour over the clam sauce and serve.

ASPARAGUS RAVIOLONI

FOR THE PASTA: (_see basic recipe on page 138_).
FOR THE FILLING: 250 g asparagus tips, 100 g fresh ricotta cheese, 100 g grated Parmesan cheese, 1 egg, salt, pepper.
FOR THE SAUCE: 40 g butter, 1 sprig rosemary, grated Parmesan cheese.

Steam the asparagus tips and keep about 20 aside for the sauce. Chop up the remainder and mix them in a bowl with the ricotta, the grated Parmesan and the egg, seasoning with salt and pepper. Blend the mixture well, then lay teaspoonfuls at regular intervals over half the sheet of rolled-out pasta. Fold over the pasta, pressing down with your fingertips around the filled sections, then cut into squares of about 4 cm.

In a small saucepan, melt and lightly colour the butter, flavouring it with the rosemary, and in another saucepan lightly sauté the remaining 20 asparagus tips.

Cook the ravioloni in plenty of boiling salted water, drain and tip them into a serving-dish. Pour over the melted butter, sprinkle with the asparagus tips and grated Parmesan, and serve.

SCALLOP RAVIOLONI

FOR THE PASTA: (_see basic recipe on page 138_).
FOR THE FILLING: 30 scallops, 2 eggs, 50 g ricotta cheese, salt, pepper.
FOR THE SAUCE: 1 ladleful tomato sauce, 1 bunch parsley, a few basil leaves, 1 clove garlic, extra-virgin olive oil, salt.

Clean the scallops under running water, put them in a casserole, cover, and open them over a lively heat. Sieve the cooking juices and set aside. Shell the scallops, eliminate the inedible parts and chop up the white flesh and the coral roe. Tip into a bowl and blend with the ricotta, eggs, salt and pepper. Arrange small heaps of the mixture over half the sheet of rolled-out pasta; fold it over, pressing down well with your fingertips between the filled sections, then cut into squares of about 4 cm.

Cook the ravioloni in plenty of salted water, drain well and tip into a serving-bowl. Pour over the sauce, garnish with a teaspoon of chopped basil and one of chopped parsley, then serve.

ZUCCHINI RAVIOLONI

◆

FOR THE PASTA: (*see basic recipe on page 138*)
FOR THE FILLING: *200 g zucchini, 150 g fresh ri-cotta cheese, grated Parmesan cheese, grated nut-meg, salt, pepper.*
FOR THE SAUCE: *4 ripe firm tomatoes, a few basil leaves, 1 leek, a few sage leaves, 40 g but-ter, extra-virgin olive oil, grated Parmesan cheese, salt, pepper.*

Clean the zucchini, slice them thinly and sauté lightly in a little butter, sea-soning with salt and grated nutmeg. Sieve and then tip them into a bowl with the ricotta and a handful of grat-ed Parmesan. Make up the ravioloni by arranging heaps of the mixture about the size of a walnut over half the sheet of rolled-out pasta; fold over the pasta and press down with your fingertips around the filled sections, then use a pastry wheel to cut out squares of about 4 cm.
Chop the leek finely and sauté in a lit-tle oil. Plunge the tomatoes into boil-ing water for a few minutes, then peel, seed and chop them and add them to the leek with a pinch of salt. Leave to reduce, and in another small saucepan melt the butter, flavouring it with a few sage leaves.
Cook the ravioloni in plenty of boiling

salted water, drain well, and tip them into a serving-dish. Pour over the tomato sauce and the melted butter and mix thoroughly. Garnish with chopped basil, sprinkle with grated Parmesan, and serve.

CHIODINI MUSHROOM
ROLL

600 g potatoes, 250 g chiodini (honey-coloured agaric or armillaria mushrooms), 200 g white flour, 100 g thinly-sliced Fontina cheese, 1 clove garlic, 1 egg, 1 glass stock, grated Parmesan cheese, 150 g butter, salt, pepper.

Set the potatoes to boil, and in the meantime clean the mushrooms with a damp cloth to remove the earthy residue. Slice them and sauté in a fry-ing-pan with 40 g of butter and the crushed garlic clove. Then add the hot stock, season with pepper and contin-ue cooking for 10 minutes. Peel and mash the potatoes, and tip them onto a floured work-surface. Add the sieved flour, the egg and a pinch of salt and knead thoroughly until you have a smooth, compact dough. Roll out into a rectangle about 1 cm thick, and cover with the slices of Fontina and the mushroom sauce. Roll up and wrap tightly in a cloth, tying it at both ends. Bring to the boil a large saucepan of salted water, immerse the roll and cook for half an hour. Once cooked, untie the cloth, place the roll on a serving-dish and cut into slices. Melt the re-maining butter, and pour it over, then sprinkle generously with Parmesan cheese. Alternatively, you can brown the sliced roll quickly in the oven dot-ted with the flaked butter.

GAME RAVIOLONI

◆

FOR THE PASTA: (*see basic recipe on page 138*).
FOR THE FILLING: 2 partridges, 2 slices smoked bacon, 50 g black truffle, 200 g spinach, grated Parmesan cheese, 1 egg, extra-virgin olive oil, 1 glass dry white wine, 1 sprig rosemary.
FOR THE SAUCE: 40 g butter, 1 clove garlic, 1 sprig rosemary, grated Parmesan cheese.

Clean, pluck and singe the partridges and remove the innards, wash carefully and dry. Wrap them with bacon and rosemary, and brown in the oil, sprinkling with white wine. When the wine has evaporated, lower the heat and complete the cooking, adding a few tablespoons of hot water from time to time if necessary. After about an hour, remove the partridges from the heat, bone them, and chop up the meat. In another saucepan, blanch the spinach briefly in a little salted water, then drain, squeeze and chop it.
In a bowl, mix together the meat, the spinach, the egg, a generous handful of grated Parmesan, the truffle (cleaned and cut in flakes), and season with salt and pepper. Arrange small heaps of the mixture over half the sheet of rolled-out pasta; fold it over, pressing down well with your fingertips between the filled sections, then cut into squares of about 4 cm.
In a small saucepan, melt and lightly colour the butter, flavouring it with a clove of garlic and a sprig of rosemary. Cook the ravioloni in plenty of boiling salted water, drain and tip them into a serving-dish. Remove the garlic and the rosemary from the melted butter and pour it over. Sprinkle generously with grated Parmesan and serve.

STROZZAPRETI
WITH OX MARROW

FOR THE PASTA: 200 g white flour, 200 g wholemeal flour, 2 eggs, 300 g spinach, salt.
FOR THE SAUCE: 150 g minced leg of veal, 80 g ox marrow, 1 small onion, 1 celery stalk, 1/2 carrot, 1 sprig rosemary, 2 bay leaves, 1 cup tomato purée, 1 glass vegetable stock, 1 glass dry white wine, grated Parmesan cheese, extra-virgin olive oil, salt, pepper.

Boil the spinach in a little salted water, squeeze and whiz in the blender. Mix the two flours in a heap in the middle of the work-surface. Make a well in the centre and break in the eggs, then add a pinch of salt and the spinach purée. Knead thoroughly with your hands until you have a smooth and elastic dough. Cover the pasta with a damp tea cloth, and leave aside for 15 minutes, then knead again, and break off with well-floured fingers pieces about the size of a hazelnut, shaping them into slightly elongated gnocchi.
Chop the carrot, celery, onion and rosemary finely, and sauté them in a saucepan in oil, together with the bay-leaf, a pinch of salt and one of pepper. Add the minced meat and the ox marrow, and brown for a few minutes, stirring all the time. Then pour over the white wine and let it evaporate. Lower the heat, add the tomato purée, and continue cooking over a low heat, adding a little hot vegetable stock from time to time.
Cook the strozzapreti in plenty of boiling salted water, drain, and tip them into the saucepan with the sauce, mixing well. Add a generous handful of grated Parmesan and serve.

SPINACH ROLL

◆

FOR THE PASTA: 250 g white flour, 2 eggs, 1 dessertspoon extra-virgin olive oil, salt.
FOR THE FILLING: 600 g spinach, 150 g fresh ricotta cheese, 100 g grated Parmesan cheese, 1 egg, red chilli pepper, extra-virgin olive oil, salt.
FOR THE SAUCE: tomato sauce, grated Parmesan cheese.

Wash the spinach carefully, boil it in a little salted water or steam, then chop finely. In a bowl, mash the ricotta with a fork, and add the spinach, the grated Parmesan and the egg. Season with salt and a pinch of chilli, then cover the bowl and set the mixture in the fridge. In the meantime, pile the flour onto a floured work-surface, make a well in the centre and break in the eggs, adding a tiny amount of water, the oil and the salt. Work thoroughly with your fingertips, and then knead with the palms of the hands until the dough is smooth, soft and elastic. Roll the dough into a large, fairly thin rectangle with a floured rolling-pin, spread with the prepared filling, and roll it up, sealing the outer edges well.
Wrap the roll in a white cloth, tying the ends carefully, and cook in a large saucepan of boiling salted water for about an hour. Serve with the tomato sauce poured over, and sprinkled with grated Parmesan.

STRANGOLAPRETI

◆

300 g spinach, 2 stale bread rolls, milk, 2 eggs, 2 dessertspoons white flour, a few sage leaves, grated Parmesan cheese, butter, salt.

Strangolapreti is a typical Alto Adige dish, and can also be prepared with nettles, spinach beet or wild spinach.
Trim the spinach carefully, wash, and steam or cook in a small amount of boiling water, then drain, squeeze and chop finely.
In the meantime crumble the bread into a bowl, moistening it with a little milk, then add the eggs, the flour and a pinch of salt and mix well. Finally add the spinach and form the mixture into gnocchi of about the size of a large walnut. Bring a large saucepan of salted water to the boil and cook the gnocchi until they come to the surface. It's best to cook the gnocchi a few at a time, to avoid the risk of them sticking together. Drain carefully, then pour over the melted butter flavoured with a few sage leaves and the grated cheese.

AUBERGINE TORTELLINI

FOR THE PASTA: (see basic recipe on page 138).
FOR THE FILLING: 200 g aubergines, 300 g ricotta cheese, a few walnuts, a few sage leaves, 1 bunch parsley, grated Parmesan cheese, extra-virgin olive oil, salt.
FOR THE SAUCE: tomato sauce, grated Parmesan cheese.

Prepare the pasta following the instructions given.
Slice the aubergines, sprinkle with

126

sea salt, and leave for about half an hour for the water to drain off. Dry, and arrange in an oiled ovenproof dish, and brown both sides in the oven. Remove the dish from the oven, leave to cool, then chop the aubergines with a half-moon chopper. Tip them into a bowl and add the ricotta, the chopped walnuts, a little Parmesan, a handful of chopped parsley and a few chopped sage leaves, and mix well.

Cut the pastry into squares, and place a small pile of the filling on each, then fold over, seal and shape into tortellini. Cook in plenty of salted water or in vegetable stock, then pour over the tomato sauce and sprinkle with Parmesan cheese.

POTATO AND SPINACH STRUGOLO

◆

1 kg potatoes, 1 kg spinach, 400 g white flour, 1 egg, grated Grana cheese, butter, salt.

Start by washing the potatoes and boiling them in their skins. In the meantime, clean and wash the spinach and either steam or cook in a little salted water. When the potatoes are cooked, peel and mash them before blending them with the flour, the egg and a pinch of salt. Then roll out the pasta about one centimetre thick on a clean damp tea cloth. Cover this with the spinach, lightly tossed in a little melted butter, then roll it up like a swiss-roll and wrap in a clean tea cloth. Tie the ends carefully with kitchen thread, and cook in a

large saucepan of salted water for about an hour. When it is cooked, remove the tea cloth and slice the strugolo. Cover the slices with a good meat sauce and sprinkle with grated Grana cheese.

CHICK PEA TORTELLI

◆

<u>FOR THE PASTA</u>: *(see basic recipe on page 138).*
<u>FOR THE FILLING</u>: *150 g chick peas, 1 onion, extra-virgin olive oil, salt.*
<u>FOR THE SAUCE</u>: *a few sage leaves, grated Parmesan cheese, butter.*

Prepare the pasta following the instructions given. If you are using dried chick peas, steep them overnight in cold water. Cook the chick peas in boiling water, drain, and purée them in a food-mill. Slice the onion, and stew in a lightly-oiled saucepan; add the chick pea purée, salt, and leave the flavours to blend. When you have switched off the heat, add enough oil to make a soft paste.

Cut the pasta into squares, place a small heap of the chick pea mixture in the middle of each, sealing and shaping each square in the normal way. Cook the tortelli in plenty of boiling salted water.

Sauté the chopped sage in plenty of butter, and use it to season the drained tortelli. Sprinkle with grated Parmesan and serve.

PUMPKIN TORTELLI

❖

40 g white flour, 1 kg bumpy yellow pumpkin, 100 g macaroons, 150 g grated Parmesan cheese, 5 eggs, butter, grated nutmeg, a few sage leaves, salt.

Remove the rind and seeds from the pumpkin and cook it in the oven. Sieve the pulp into a bowl and blend in one egg, the crumbled macaroons and the grated Parmesan, seasoning with salt and nutmeg. Mix the flour with the remaining eggs and a pinch of salt, kneading well until you have a firm, even dough. Roll out into a thin sheet then cut into squares. Place a little of the pumpkin filling in the centre of each, then fold over the pasta sealing the edges well.

Melt the butter, flavouring it with a few sage leaves. Cook the tortelli in plenty of boiling salted water, drain, and serve, with the flavoured butter poured over and sprinkled with grated Parmesan.

In Lombardy the filling is made with the addition of about 100 g of Cremona mustard (candied fruit in a mustard syrup), with the fruit finely chopped and blended with its own syrup.

TORTELLINI
WITH MEAT FILLING

❖

FOR THE PASTA: *(see basic recipe on page 138).*
FOR THE FILLING: *100 g chicken breast, 100 g pork loin, 100 g veal, 150 g Parma ham, 1 fairly thick slice Mortadella sausage, 100 g grated Parmesan cheese, 2 eggs, butter, nutmeg, salt, pepper.*

Mince the meat and brown in a saucepan with a knob of butter, then tip it into a bowl with the chopped ham and the chopped mortadella. Blend together with the 2 eggs, add the grated Parmesan, and season with a pinch of grated nutmeg, salt and pepper.
Prepare the pasta following the instructions given, then roll out into a thin sheet, and cut into squares of about 4 - 5 cm (as you become more expert you will be able to make the tortellini even smaller) and pile a little of the filling on each one. Fold the opposite corners together to form a triangle, seal the edges well, then roll around your finger and pinch the two ends together, turning the upper edge outwards.
Cook the tortellini in boiling salted water, or better still in hot meat stock, then drain and serve with a meat sauce, or if you prefer simply with melted butter flavoured with a few sage leaves.

129

TORTELLONI
WITH VEGETARIAN FILLING

❖

FOR THE PASTA: *(see basic recipe on page 138).*
FOR THE FILLING: *350 g spinach beet, 250 g ricotta cheese, salt, pepper.*
FOR THE SAUCE: *a few sage leaves, grated Parmesan cheese, butter.*

Prepare the pasta following the instructions given. Trim the spinach beet, and boil in a little salted water, then chop and tip into a bowl with the ricotta which you have beaten into a smooth cream. Blend well, and season with salt and pepper.

Roll out the pasta into a thin sheet. Place the filling in small heaps at regular intervals over half the pasta. Fold over the other half, then cut the tortelloni into the desired shape using the special cutters, and seal the edges well. Cook the tortelloni in plenty of boiling water, drain, and tip into a serving-dish. Pour over the melted butter flavoured with a few sage leaves, and sprinkle with grated Parmesan. These tortelloni are also excellent served with a light tomato sauce.

POTATO TORTELLONI

FOR THE PASTA: 500 g wheatmeal flour, 200 g floury potatoes, 3 eggs, salt.
FOR THE FILLING: 400 g mixed cheese (Ricotta, Gorgonzola, Emmental etc.).
FOR THE SAUCE: grated Parmesan cheese, butter.

Boil the potatoes, then peel and mash them, and mix them with the flour. Blend in the eggs, a pinch of salt and a little of the potato cooking water and knead into a pliable dough. Roll out on a floured work-surface, and cut into strips of about 10 cm. In the lower half of each strip place small piles of the finely-diced cheeses at regular intervals. Fold over the pasta, pressing the edges down well, and cut out the tortelloni using the special cutter, or a glass with a slightly moistened rim.
Bring a large saucepan of salted water

to the boil, drop in the tortelloni and cook briefly. Drain and tip onto a warm serving-dish, pour over the melted butter, sprinkle with grated Parmesan and serve.

TORTELLONI WITH SPINACH AND RICOTTA FILLING

FOR THE PASTA: (see basic recipe on page 138).
FOR THE FILLING: 300 g spinach, 300 g ricotta cheese, 1 bunch parsley, 2 eggs, grated nutmeg, 50 g grated Parmesan cheese, salt, pepper.
FOR THE SAUCE: a few sage leaves, 100 g grated Parmesan cheese, butter.

Prepare the pasta following the instructions given.
Sieve the ricotta, boil the spinach in a little salted water, drain, squeeze thoroughly and chop. Tip both into a bowl, and blend in the eggs, the chopped parsley and the grated Parmesan, seasoning the mixture with salt, pepper and a pinch of grated nutmeg. Mix all the ingredients to a smooth cream. Roll out the pasta into a thin sheet and cut out disks of about 8 cm. Place a small ball of the filling in the centre of each, then fold in half to form half-moon shapes, sealing the edges well. Cook in plenty of boiling salted water, and when they are ready, serve with the melted butter flavoured with a few sage leaves. Sprinkle generously with grated Parmesan and serve immediately.

HOME MADE PASTA

HOW TO COLOUR FRESH PASTA

If you want to make coloured pasta, here are a few suggestions:
- **yellow**: add a pinch of powdered saffron to the dough;
- **orange**: make up the dough using only two eggs, and adding 400 g yellow pumpkin prepared as follows – peel, seed and steam the pumpkin, then sieve the pulp, drying it out in a saucepan over the heat if it is too watery;
- **red**: make up the dough using only 3 eggs and adding 3 dessertspoons of tomato concentrate diluted in a little water;
- **green**: make up the dough using only 2 eggs and adding 200 g of boiled, squeezed and finely-chopped spinach.
- **brown**: add 50-60 g unsweetened cocoa powder to the dough;
- **black**: make up the dough using only 3 eggs and add the sieved contents of 2 cuttlefish ink sacs diluted in a little white wine.

133

PASTA
WITHOUT EGGS

CAVATIEDDI
◆

200 g extrafine flour, 100 g wheatflour, water, salt.

Mix the two types of flour and tip onto a floured work-surface, then blend well with a pinch of salt dissolved in a little warm water.
Knead thoroughly until you have a smooth, soft dough, then roll into long sausages about 1/2 cm thick, and cut into maccheroni-length pieces.
Flatten each cylinder with a round-bladed knife to create small elongated shell shapes, then lay them out to dry on a floured tea cloth.

FETTUCCINE
◆

400 g durum wheat flour, 10 g extra-virgin olive oil, water, salt.

Pour the flour onto a work-surface, make a well in the middle and pour in the oil, a little warm water and a pinch of salt. Knead vigorously, adding more water gradually as required. Then roll into a ball and leave aside for half an hour. Roll out the pasta as thinly as possible, and leave it to dry, covered, on a wooden board, then cut out the fettucine strips about 1 cm wide.

MALLOREDDUS
◆

400 g durum wheat flour, white flour as required, 1 pinch saffron, water, salt.

HOW TO COOK FRESH PASTA

Fresh pasta must be cooked in plenty of salted water. The recommended amount of water is about eight times the weight of the pasta. A spoonful of oil added to the water prevents the pasta sticking together. It is essential to drop in the pasta when the water is already boiling, stirring gently with a wooden fork so that it does not stick to the bottom or stick together in lumps.

Filled pasta should, on the other hand, be dropped into the water just before it comes to the boil, to prevent the shapes opening and the filling spilling out.

When you drop in the pasta the water stops boiling, so you must turn up the heat to bring it back to the boil. Once the water is boiling again, regulate the heat so that it continues to boil gently. Never cover the boiling saucepan completely or the water will boil over. Cooking times depend on the type of pasta, the thickness, the various ingredients used (egg, different types of flour etc), and on individual taste. We nevertheless recommend draining the pasta while it still has "bite" or is, as the Italians say, "al dente".

Filled pasta has to be cooked with particular care, because if it is cooked too long or over too violent a heat, the pasta shapes may split or break open.

It is also important that the water used for cooking the pasta is not too calcareous, since hard water can obstruct the natural porosity of the pasta so that it does not cook evenly. This problem can be easily resolved by fitting the water supply with a special filter.

Dissolve the saffron and the salt in a cup of water, and blend this into the wheat flour on a floured work-surface. Knead the pasta, adding as much white flour as necessary to produce a soft, smooth dough. Roll the pasta out into long sausages about 1/2 cm thick and cut into 2cm lengths.

The malloreddus are traditionally marked using a special bamboo tool, but if you haven't got one you can push them over the back of a grater like gnocchi to produce a similar effect. Then leave them to dry on floured tea cloths in a fairly cool place.

ORECCHIETTE

♦

160 g extrafine flour, 240 g durum wheat flour, water, salt.

Mix the two flours on a work-surface, add a pinch of salt, and enough water to mix and knead to a smooth, elastic dough. Work thoroughly for about ten minutes, then roll the dough out into long sausages and cut into lengths of about 1 centimetre. Using a round-bladed knife, flatten each cylinder into a shell-shape on the floured work-surface, then form into "little ears" by moulding them over the tip of your thumb, and lay to dry on lightly-floured tea cloths.

PICI

♦

400 g extrafine flour, extra-virgin olive oil, water, salt.

This typical Sienese pasta is a type of home-made spaghetti. The pici are made by hand and rolled out on the chopping-board, and the most expert housewives can roll them out up to two metres long! Tip the flour into the centre of the work-surface, add 1 dessertspoon of extra-virgin olive oil, a pinch of salt, and enough water to mix the dough. Knead energetically, adding a little warm water gradually if required. When you have a firm, smooth dough, roll into a ball, brush the surface with oil, and leave to rest covered with a tea-cloth for about half an hour. Then roll out into a sheet about 1.5 cm thick and cut into thin 3mm strips, rolling them out with well-floured hands into a spaghetti shape. As you prepare them, lay the pici out to dry on a tea cloth dusted with flour or semolina to prevent them sticking together.

HOW TO STORE FRESH PASTA

In the fridge. The ideal temperature for storing fresh and filled pasta is 3 or 4°C. Don't cover it with clingfilm or keep it closed in plastic containers, as the pasta has to "breathe". It is best stored in special paper or cardboard food containers, or better still on a ceramic plate covered with a cotton cloth.
Out of the fridge: We advise strongly against storing the pasta out of the fridge, especially filled pasta, since high temperatures or changes in temperature can accelerate the deterioration of the ingredients. As well as this, in the case of filled pasta, the fats included in the filling will tend to leak out on to the pasta case.

PISAREI

◆

300 g extrafine flour, 100 g breadcrumbs, water, salt.

Blanch the breadcrumbs in a small amount of boiling water, then blend with the flour on the work-surface, adding a pinch of salt and enough water to mix the dough. Knead thoroughly with your hands until you have a firm, smooth, elastic dough. Divide the dough into balls, and roll these out into sausages about 1/2 cm thick, then cut into lengths of about 1.5 cm. Then use your thumb to mould the cylinders into shell-shapes.

PIZZOCCHERI

◆

250 g buckwheat flour, 150 g extrafine flour, water, salt, pepper.

Mix the two flours on a floured work-surface, then add a pinch of salt and enough water to blend. Knead thoroughly with your hands until you have a firm, elastic dough. With a rolling-pin, roll out a sheet about 1.5 mm thick, and cut into strips about 1 cm wide and 7 cm long.

SPAGHETTI
ALLA CHITARRA

◆

400 g extrafine flour, 2 dessertspoons lard, water, salt.

Rub the lard into the flour and add the salt and enough water to make a firm, elastic dough. Knead thoroughly, then roll out a sheet of the same thickness as that between the wires of the "guitar".
The *chitarra* or guitar is an instrument made up of a wooden frame strung with wires used for cutting spaghetti. The sheet of pasta is laid on top then pressed through by rolling over it with the rolling pin.
If you do not have a "guitar", use the draw-plate of the pasta machine which is normally used for tagliolini. When you have finished, lay out the spaghetti to dry on a floured tea cloth.

TROFIE

◆

400 g extrafine flour, water, salt.

Pour the flour onto the work-surface, add a pinch of salt and enough water to mix. Knead thoroughly with your hands until you have a dense, smooth, elastic dough.
Break off pieces about the size of a bean, roll them into thin sausages then, with well-floured hands, twist them into corkscrew shapes. Leave them to dry on a flour-sprinkled tea-cloth for four hours before cooking.

Egg pasta

Bigoli

◆

250 g extrafine flour, 150 g durum wheat flour, 4 eggs, water, salt.

Pile the two types of flour in the centre of the work-surface, make a well in the centre and break in the eggs and add a pinch of salt. Work the eggs in to the flour, adding a little water if the mixture is too dry. Knead thoroughly until you have a smooth, elastic dough.
Put the dough into the pasta mill, using a wheel with 3mm holes, then cut the bigoli into lengths of 20cm with a knife. Leave the pasta to dry on a floured tea cloth for several hours before using.

Filatieddi

◆

400 g extrafine flour, 4 eggs, 1 dessertspoon extra-virgin olive oil, salt.

Pour the flour onto the work-surface. Make a well in the centre and break in the eggs, add a pinch of salt and the oil, and beat them with a fork. Then rub in with your fingertips, and knead the pasta until you have a firm dough. Shape it into a ball, wrap it up in a tea cloth, moistened in warm water and well-wrung, and leave aside for about 30 minutes.
Roll the pasta out with the rolling-pin into two sheets, and cut them into squares, then shape them into little wheels

with your fingers. As you prepare them, lay them out on a floured tray, and leave to rest for a few minutes.

Garganelli

◆

250 g extrafine flour, 150 g durum wheat flour, 2 whole eggs and 1 yolk, salt.

Mix the two types of flour on the work-surface, then make a well in the centre and break in 2 whole eggs and 1 yolk and a pinch of salt. Mix thoroughly, and knead until you have a smooth, elastic dough. Use a rolling-pin to roll out a sheet about 1mm thick, and cut into 6cm squares. Roll these up diagonally around a wooden stick about the size of a pencil, pressing them with your fingertips. Then mark the garganelli using the special tool known as a comb, remove, and lay them out to dry.

Pasta base
for cannelloni

◆

500 g extrafine flour, 4 eggs, 1 dessertspoon extra-virgin olive oil, salt.

Pour the flour onto the work-surface, make a well in the centre and break in the eggs, adding a pinch of salt and a dessertspoon of extra-virgin olive oil. Rub in well, then knead until you have a smooth, elastic dough. Leave covered in a damp tea cloth for about half an hour, then knead again, and roll out sheets about 1 mm thick with a rolling-pin. Use a knife to cut the pasta into squares of about 12cm.
Cook the squares of pasta a few at a time, draining them while they are still al dente and then lay them out singly on a damp tea cloth to dry.

PASTA BASE
FOR LASAGNE

◆

500 g extrafine flour, 4 eggs, 1 dessertspoon extra-virgin olive oil, salt.

Add the eggs to the flour along with a pinch of salt and a dessertspoon of extra-virgin olive oil. Mix well, and knead thoroughly with your hands until you have a smooth and elastic dough. Leave covered with a damp tea cloth for about half an hour, then knead again and roll out a sheet about 1.5 mm thick. Leave to rest for about 15 minutes, then with a knife cut out squares of about 10 cm (the size can be varied according to requirements). Dry out for at least a couple of hours before cooking. Cook the lasagne a few at a time, draining them while they are still *al dente* and then lay them out singly on a damp tea cloth to dry.

PASTA BASE
FOR FRESH FILLED PASTA

◆

400 g extrafine flour, 4 eggs, 1 dessertspoon extra-virgin olive oil, salt.

Pour the flour onto the work surface, add the eggs, a little salt and the oil. Mix thoroughly, kneading until you have a smooth, elastic dough. Leave covered with a damp tea cloth for about half an hour, then knead again and roll out thin sheets with the rolling-pin. This pasta is much easier to work with if it is not allowed to dry out.

TAGLIATELLE, TAGLIOLINI, FETTUCCINE, PAPPARDELLE

◆

500 g extrafine flour, 4 eggs, 1 dessertspoon extra-virgin olive oil, 1 handful maize meal.

Pour the flour into the middle of a work-surface, make a well in the centre and add the eggs with a pinch of salt and the oil, blend in well, and knead thoroughly with your hands until you have a smooth and elastic dough. Leave covered with a damp tea cloth for half an hour, then knead again and roll out into thin sheets with the rolling-pin. Sprinkle with the maize meal and leave to rest for a few minutes, then roll out and cut into strips of the desired width. Tagliatelle are 2cm wide, fettucine 1 cm, tagliolini a few millimetres, and pappardelle 3 or 4 cm.

SAUCES AND DRESSING

GARLIC BUTTER

◆

150 g butter, 50 g garlic cloves, a few basil leaves.

Chop the garlic and the basil very finely. In a bowl, mix the seasonings with the softened butter and beat to a cream. Wrap it up in aluminium foil and put it in the fridge to harden.
If the pieces of garlic are too easily visible, push the creamy mixture through a fine-mesh sieve before setting it to harden. Another tip for making sure the garlic is not obtrusively visible in the butter is to blanch the cloves for a few seconds in boiling water before chopping so that they remain white. Ideal for seasoning pasta and rice dishes.

TRUFFLE BUTTER

◆

150 g butter, 100 g white truffles, salt.

In a bowl beat the butter to a cream, then add the truffles which you have cleaned and crushed in a mortar. Blend the two ingredients well with a pestle or a wooden spoon, and season with a pinch of salt.
Wrap the butter up in aluminium foil and store in the fridge. Excellent with plain boiled pasta.

BASIL OIL

◆

1 l extra-virgin olive oil, 1 handful basil florets, 10 basil leaves.

Gather the basil florets in the morning, leaving them to dry in the sun-light if they are veiled in dew, and place them in a hermetically-sealed container.
Pour in the oil, close and leave to macerate for 3 weeks in a dark, cool place. Then add the basil leaves and replace the container for another week. Finally filter, and decant into small bottles. This is an excellent condiment for use both with hot pasta dishes and pasta salads.

GARLIC OIL

◆

1 l oil, 6 large cloves fresh garlic or 4 cloves mature garlic.

Peel the garlic cloves, press them lightly with the back of a knife-blade, place them in a hermetically-sealed container and pour the oil over them.
Close and store in a cool, dark place for about 20 days. Finally, filter, and use to dress pasta salads.

CHILLI OIL

◆

1 l extra-virgin olive oil, 3 or 4 red chilli peppers, 1 bay leaf.

Crumble the chilli peppers and the bay leaf and place them in a hermetically-sealed container, covering them with the oil. Leave to infuse for about a month in a cool, dark place, and then filter. For a spicier flavour simply leave the oil to infuse for longer, while if you prefer a lighter taste you can dilute the flavoured oil with a little fresh oil. Particularly recommended for dressing pasta salads.

BÉCHAMEL

50 g butter, 50 g flour, 1/2 l milk, 1 pinch grated nutmeg, salt, pepper.

The correct preparation of a béchamel sauce is one of the first hurdles to be faced by any cook. The fear of ending up with a lumpy, tasteless liquid will be gradually overcome with experience and by learning from mistakes. All it takes is practice, and after a number of attempts you will soon discover that you too can make a smooth and tasty béchamel, without even needing to measure the ingredients.

In a casserole, melt the butter gently over a low flame. Sprinkle the flour over it, and beat it in using an egg-whisk.

141

Heat the milk, without letting it boil, and use it to dilute the sauce; the milk should be added gradually, stirring all the time, to avoid the formation of the much-dreaded lumps.

Continue stirring rhythmically until you can feel the sauce thickening, and as soon as the first boiling bubbles begin to form, count 10 minutes cooking-time, stirring all the time. Just before you switch off the heat, add salt, a grind of fresh pepper and a pinch of grated nutmeg.

Should you require a thicker sauce you can increase the quantities of butter and flour (always the same amount of each) and use the normal amount of milk, or you can thicken the sauce further over the heat at the time of boiling. Should you desire a particularly light sauce, you can substitute the milk with vegetable stock, or with fish fumet for use with fish-based dishes.

GENOESE PESTO

◆

1 handful basil leaves, 1 clove garlic, 2 dessert-spoons pine-nuts, 1 dessertspoon grated Pecorino cheese, 1 dessertspoon grated Parmesan cheese, ex-tra-virgin olive oil, salt.

Wash and dry the basil leaves and put them in a stone mortar with the garlic and the pine-nuts (reduce the basil leaves by pressing them against the sides of the mortar with the pestle, without actually pounding them). Continue grinding the ingredients, then add the grated cheeses and a pinch of salt.
As soon as you have a smooth paste, add as much olive oil as required, stirring with the pestle like a spoon, until you have a thick, creamy sauce. When using the pesto, dilute it with a few spoonfuls of the pasta cooking water. If you prefer, this sauce can also be successfully made in a blender.
Pesto goes perfectly with all types of pasta, rice, gnocchi and minestrone. It can be stored in the fridge in hermetically-sealed glass jars, covering the surface with a thin layer of oil, and without the cheeses which should be added fresh at the moment of use.

PINZIMONIO WITH ROCKET AND PARMESAN CHEESE

◆

5 dessertspoons extra-virgin olive oil, 2 dessert-spoons lemon juice, 1/2 bunch rocket, 1 clove garlic, Parmesan cheese, salt, pepper.

Carefully blend the oil with the lemon juice and a pinch of salt, then add the finely-chopped rocket and garlic, and season with a twist of freshly-ground pepper. Finally add small flakes of

Parmesan to the sauce, mixing carefully so as not to break up the flakes of cheese too much. Use this sauce to season plain pasta dishes.

MEAT SAUCE WITH BALSAMIC VINEGAR

◆

400 g veal, 100 g bacon, 1 handful dried mushrooms, 3 peeled tomatoes, 2 celery stalks, 1 onion, 1 carrot, 2 bay leaves, 1 pinch powdered cinnamon, 50 g butter, 2 dessertspoons of balsamic vinegar, salt, freshly-ground pepper.

Clean and chop the celery stalks, the onion and the carrot, then tip them into a saucepan, add the bacon and the butter and gently sauté the ingredients, stirring all the time with a wooden spoon. Wash the mushrooms, and steep them in warm water and chop the veal into pieces. When the vegetables and the meat are gently browned, tip in the mashed tomatoes, add the meat, and leave the flavours to blend over a moderate heat. Finally add the well-drained mushrooms, the cinnamon and the bay-leaves. Season with salt, freshly-ground pepper and the balsamic vinegar, and leave to cook for about an hour over a moderate heat, stirring every so often.

BASS SAUCE

◆

250 g bass meat, 200 g ripe, firm tomatoes, 15 g fresh dill, 1 clove garlic, 1 dl cream, dry white wine, extra-virgin olive oil, salt.

In a saucepan, flavour a few dessertspoons of oil with the finely-chopped garlic, then add the chopped fish, and the diced dill.

142

Leave the fish to absorb the flavours for a few minutes, then pour over the white wine, and let it evaporate. Plunge the tomatoes into boiling water for a few minutes, peel, seed and chop them and tip them into the saucepan. Leave to reduce, then dilute with the cream, season with salt, and continue cooking until the sauce has the correct consistency.

GROUPER SAUCE

◆

800 g grouper slices, 400 g tomato sauce, 1 onion, 1 carrot, 1/2 celery stalk, 1 clove garlic, 1 chilli pepper, 1 bunch parsley, basil, 1/2 glass wine, extra-virgin olive oil.

Clean the fish, removing the skin and any bones. Chop the garlic, celery, onion and carrot finely, and sauté them in a saucepan in a few dessertspoons of oil, along with the crumbled chilli. Place two slices of fish in the saucepan, pour over the white wine and let it evaporate, then break up the fish meat, blending it in with the rest of the sauce. Pour over the tomato sauce, season with salt and continue cooking for about twenty minutes. Ten minutes before the end of cooking, add the rest of the fish, and let it absorb the juices, turning the slices over frequently, then remove them with a slatted spoon and set aside. Use the sauce over pasta drained while it is still *al dente*, sprinkling with chopped parsley and basil. Serve garnished with the pieces of fish.

TOMATO SAUCE

◆

800 g ripe firm tomatoes, 1 bunch parsley, 1/2 teaspoon sugar, extra-virgin olive oil, salt, red chilli pepper.

This is the classic tomato sauce, pummarola, the sauce *par excellence* for serving with pasta.
Wash the tomatoes, then plunge them in boiling water to make them easier to peel, remove the skin, the stalks and the seeds and pass them through the food-mill. If the tomatoes are very watery, it is best to leave them to drain on a sloping surface for at least 15 minutes before puréeing them.
Put the tomato purée in a saucepan over a moderate heat, adding a dash of oil, and reduce for about 30 minutes, seasoning with salt and the half-teaspoon of sugar (to counteract the natural acidity).
Just before switching off the heat, season with chilli pepper and chopped basil.

Variation
800 g ripe firm tomatoes, 4 cloves garlic, 1 bunch parsley, oregano (optional), extra-virgin olive oil, red chilli pepper, salt.

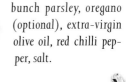

Peel and purée the tomatoes as in the preceding recipe. In a saucepan, flavour a few dessertspoons of oil with the crushed garlic, being careful not to let the garlic burn or to overheat the oil (as otherwise the tomato would burn when added). Lower the heat, and add the tomato (if you wish you can remove the garlic at this stage, if you do not like its strong flavour), then cover the pan and continue cooking. After about 20 minutes season with salt, chilli pepper, chopped parsley and, if you wish, a pinch of oregano.

ASPARAGUS SAUCE

◆

2 bunches asparagus, 1 dessertspoon lemon juice, 2.5 dl milk, grated nutmeg, oil, salt, pepper.

Trim the asparagus and cut the tips and the tender parts of the stems into small pieces, then sauté them in a few dessertspoons of oil, season with salt, pepper

and grated nutmeg and add a little less than half a glass of hot water. Cover, and cook over a moderate heat for about 15 minutes. As soon as the water has dried out, add the lemon juice. Cook the asparagus until they are quite soft, adding the milk gradually. Whiz in the blender, then heat up again.

ARTICHOKE SAUCE

◆

7 artichokes, 50 g salted capers, 50 g black olives, 2 cloves garlic, the juice of 1 lemon, 1 bunch parsley, oregano, 3 dessertspoons breadcrumbs, 1 dessertspoon tamari sauce, extra-virgin olive oil, salt, pepper.

Cut off the stalks and the tips of the artichokes and remove the tougher outside leaves. Cut into wedges and steep for a few minutes in water mixed with a little lemon juice. Drain and blanch for 10 minutes in salted water with lemon juice, then drain again and chop. Chop the garlic and parsley finely and mix with the breadcrumbs, then sauté in a saucepan in a couple of dessertspoons of oil. After a few minutes add the artichokes, mix, and then add the stoned olives, the capers rinsed of their salt and dried, the tamari sauce, 1 glass of water and a twist of freshly-ground pepper. Lower the flame, and cook with the lid on for about 30 minutes, stirring every so often.
When cooking is complete, adjust salt to taste (you probably won't need to add any because of the tamari sauce), and season with a little oregano.

ZUCCHINI FLOWER SAUCE

◆

12 zucchini flowers, 1/2 onion, 1 bunch parsley, 1 pinch saffron powder, 1 egg yolk, grated Pecorino cheese, extra-virgin olive oil, salt, pepper.

Heat a few tablespoons of oil in a saucepan, then add the finely chopped zucchini flowers, parsley and onion, the saffron dissolved in a ladleful of hot water, and a pinch of salt and pepper. Cook over a moderate heat for about 15 minutes, mixing all the time, then whiz in a blender or put through the food-mill.
Tip the resulting purée back into the saucepan, dilute with a little oil, and heat up thoroughly. Turn off the heat, cool slightly, then blend in the egg yolk and a few tablespoons of grated Pecorino cheese.

PEPPER SAUCE

◆

4 green and yellow peppers, 1 onion, 1 clove garlic, 1 bunch parsley, dry white wine, extra-virgin olive oil, salt, pepper.

Wash the peppers, remove the

stalks, seeds and inner membranes, and dice. In a saucepan, soften the chopped onion in a little oil, add the peppers and sauté, stirring all the time with a wooden spoon. Pour over a little wine, let it evaporate, season with salt and lower the heat, then cover the pan and stew slowly for about twenty minutes. Just before switching off, add the chopped basil, the finely sliced garlic, a twist of freshly ground pepper and a dash of olive oil.

SEA-URCHIN SAUCE

◆

30 sea-urchins, 400 g ripe firm tomatoes, 1 onion, 2 cloves garlic, 1 bunch parsley, pinch saffron, extra-virgin olive oil, salt, pepper.

Clean the sea urchins, removing the inner part with the help of a tea-spoon. Chop the onion finely, sauté in plenty of oil and then add the toma-toes (plunged in boiling water, peeled, seeded and roughly chopped). Dilute the saffron in a ladleful of hot water or stock and pour it over, then season with salt and pepper. Continue cooking for 15 minutes over a low heat, then add the sea-urchin meat and a very finely chopped mixture of parsley and gar-lic. Switch off when the tomato is cooked, adding a little hot water or stock if the sauce seems too dry.

145

THREE CHEESES SAUCE

◆

100 g Gorgonzola, 100 g Fontina, 100 g Gruyère, 1/2 glass cream, béchamel (see page 141), butter, pepper, grated nutmeg, salt.

Prepare a fairly liquid béchamel sauce and, as soon as it is cooked, stir in the diced cheeses, the cream, a knob of butter, a pinch of salt, a twist of freshly ground pepper, and a sprinkle of grated nutmeg. Continue to heat until you have a fluid, creamy sauce, then switch off. Add a little grated Parmesan to make this into the classic "4 cheeses" sauce.

FISHERMAN'S SAUCE

◆

200 g clams, 200 g mussels, 200 g shrimps, 8 scallops, 3 ripe, firm tomatoes, 1 clove garlic, chives, 1 bunch parsley, 2 dessertspoons extra-virgin olive oil, red chilli pepper, salt.

Clean the different types of fish carefully. Steep the mussels and clams in salty water for at least half an hour, then place them in a frying-pan and open them over a rapid heat. Remove the shellfish from their shells and sieve the cooking juices which have accumulated in the bottom of the pan. Open the scallops and remove the flesh, eliminating the inedible parts and setting the white flesh and the coral roes aside, and shell the shrimps. Flavour a few spoonfuls of oil with the crushed garlic clove; as soon as it turns golden, remove the garlic and add the peeled, seeded and roughly chopped tomatoes, and a crumbled chilli pepper without its seeds. After a few minutes add the scallops, mussels, clams and shrimps, pouring over the sieved shellfish cooking juices. Season with salt and continue cooking for another 5-6 minutes. Before switching off, sprinkle with chopped chives and parsley. If you are using the sauce over pasta,

stir it into the saucepan and blend carefully, coating the pasta thoroughly with sauce.

TROUT (OR TENCH) SAUCE

◆

1 400 g trout (or tench), 200 g tomato sauce, 1 small onion, 1 clove garlic, 1 sprig marjoram, 1 bunch parsley, extra-virgin olive oil, salt, red chilli pepper.

Clean the trout and cook for 10 minutes in boiling salted water, bone it, and chop the flesh into small pieces. Chop the onion, garlic and marjoram finely and sauté in a saucepan with a few dessertspoons of oil and a few small pieces of crumbled chilli. Add the tomato sauce, season with salt and leave to reduce over a moderate heat. After this, add the trout meat, and cook slowly allowing the flavours to blend for about 15 minutes. Before switching off, sprinkle with finely chopped parsley.

SEAFOOD SAUCE

◆

200 g cockles, 200 g mussels, 100 g monkfish, 100 g baby squid, 100 g cuttlefish, 3 prawns, 2 shrimps, 1/2 onion, 3 cloves garlic, basil, ginger, 2 glasses dry white wine, extra-virgin olive oil, salt, pepper.

Chop the onion and garlic finely, and sauté in a saucepan in plenty of oil. Clean the squid and the cuttlefish, chop them into pieces and tip into the saucepan with the monkfish meat. Open the cockles and mussels in a frying-pan over a fairly rapid heat, shell most of them, and add them to the sauce. Last of all add the prawns and the shrimps. Do not overcook, but just sauté lightly before pouring over the white wine, letting it evaporate over a rapid heat. Season with salt, lower the heat, and finish cooking, adding the chopped basil and a little freshly grated ginger just before you switch off the heat.

TOMATO AND OLIVE SAUCE

◆

500 g ripe, firm tomatoes, 150 g black and green olives, 2 dessertspoons of salted capers, 1 clove garlic, oregano or basil, extra-virgin olive oil, red chilli pepper, salt.

Plunge the tomatoes into boiling water for a few minutes, then peel, seed and chop them. Chop the garlic finely and sauté in a saucepan with a few spoonfuls of oil, adding the tomatoes before it browns. Then add the green olives stoned and chopped, the black olives stoned but whole, and the capers with the salt rinsed off under running water and dried. Season with salt and cook over a moderate heat. Just before you switch off the heat add the oregano (or the chopped basil) and a dash of oil.

EEL AND PEA SAUCE

◆

200 g cleaned eel, 200 g freshly podded peas, 1 onion, 1 cup tomato sauce, 1 clove garlic, 1 bay leaf, extra-virgin olive oil, salt.

Cut the eel into pieces, chop the onion and sauté both in a saucepan in a few dessertspoons of oil. As soon as they are evenly coloured, add the tomato sauce and the bay leaf, and after a little stir in the podded peas and the garlic. Finish cooking the sauce, and serve with pasta or polenta.

CHESTNUT AND SAUSAGE SAUCE

◆

20 g ground chestnuts, 200 g sausage, 4 egg yolks, 1/4 l cream, extra-virgin olive oil, salt, pepper.

Peel the sausage, break up the meat with a fork, and sauté gently in a saucepan in a few spoonfuls of oil, making sure that it remains soft. Dissolve the ground chestnuts in the cream, and pour in with the sausage meat. In a warmed soup tureen blend the egg yolks with a pinch of salt and pepper, and when the pasta is cooked and drained, tip it in and mix well. Then pour over the heated sausage and cream sauce, stirring it in well, and serve sprinkled with grated Parmesan.

BEAN SAUCE

◆

250 g boiled Borlotti beans, 50 g fatty bacon, 300 g tomato pulp, 1/2 onion, 1 carrot, 1/2 celery stalk, 1 clove garlic, 1 bunch parsley, a few basil leaves, extra-virgin olive oil, salt, pepper.

Chop the bacon along with the parsley and garlic, then sauté in a saucepan in a few spoonfuls of oil. Chop the carrot, celery and onion finely and tip into the pan, and after about 10 minutes add the beans. Stir gently, letting the flavours blend, then add the tomato pulp, season with salt and pepper, cover, lower the heat and continue cooking. Just before you switch off, season with a few roughly chopped basil leaves and a little chopped parsley.

ARTICHOKE, MUSHROOM AND RICOTTA SAUCE

◆

250 g fresh ricotta cheese, 4 artichokes, 200 g fresh mushrooms, 1 shallot, 1 clove garlic, 1 bunch parsley, juice of 1 lemon, 1 dessertspoon tomato concentrate (optional), grated Parmesan cheese, dry white wine, extra-virgin olive oil, salt, pepper.

Clean the artichokes, cut off the tips and most of the stalks and remove the tougher outside leaves. Cut into thin wedges and steep in water mixed with a little lemon juice. Clean the mushrooms, removing the earthy residue with a damp cloth, and cut into thin slices. Chop the garlic and shallot finely, and sauté in a saucepan in a few spoonfuls of oil, then add the artichokes and the mushrooms and let the flavours blend, stirring all the time over a rapid heat.

After a few minutes, lower the heat, pour over a little white wine and let it evaporate. Season with salt and pepper, cover the saucepan and continue cooking for about 20 minutes. Add a little hot water if necessary and, if you choose to use it, the tomato concentrate dissolved in a little hot water.

When the sauce is cooked add the crumbled ricotta, a few dessertspoons of grated Parmesan and a sprinkle of finely chopped parsley. Mix thoroughly and let the cheeses melt slightly before switching off the heat.

CAULIFLOWER OR BROCCOLI SAUCE

1 cauliflower, or a similar quantity of broccoli, 1 onion, 1 dessertspoon of raisins, 1 dessertspoon pine-nuts, 2 salted anchovies (optional) grated Pecorino cheese, extra-virgin olive oil, red chilli pepper, salt.

Either cauliflower or broccoli can be used for this sauce; if you use the latter you must then serve with pasta orechiette to reproduce the classic dish from Puglia.

Steep the raisins in a little warm water. Remove the florets from the cauliflower and blanch them in boiling salted water. Chop the onion and sauté in a saucepan in a few spoonfuls of oil, then add the anchovies with the salt rinsed off (if you choose to use them), stirring them in until they disintegrate. Add the cauliflower or broccoli florets and continue cooking until they are tender, adding a little hot water if necessary. Before switching off the heat, adjust salt to taste, season with chilli pepper and add the pine-nuts and the drained and dried raisins.

To serve, tip the pasta into the sauce and mix gently, then sprinkle with grated Pecorino cheese, or if you are using fresh Pecorino, dice it instead.

SOLE SAUCE

◆

300 g sole fillets, 1 handful basil leaves, white flour as required, 1 dl cream, 1 small measure cognac, meat stock, butter, salt, pepper.

Coat the sole fillets lightly in flour and brown them gently in the butter in a frying-pan. As soon as they are nicely-

coloured, pour over the cognac and 2 ladlefuls of hot stock. As soon as the sauce begins to reduce, dilute it with the cream, sprinkle with basil, and adjust salt and pepper to taste. Tip the drained pasta into the sauce, mixing it in well before serving garnished with a few fresh basil leaves.

HAM AND PEA SAUCE

200 g small podded peas, 1/2 onion, 2 eggs, 4 dessertspoons grated Parmesan cheese, 100 g thinly-sliced cooked ham, extra-virgin olive oil, salt, pepper.

Chop the onion finely and sauté in a saucepan in a few dessertspoons of oil, then add the peas, salt and pepper. Lower the heat, cover, and cook until the peas are tender, adding a little hot water if necessary. Cut the ham into small strips and add to the peas just before you switch off the heat, allowing the flavours to blend. In a soup-tureen mix the eggs with the Parmesan, a pinch of salt and a twist of freshly-ground pepper. When the pasta is cooked, drain and tip into the tureen, mixing well, then pour over the pea and ham sauce and stir it in gently.

150

EGG AND MOZZARELLA SAUCE

◆

4 eggs, 1/2 onion, 1 mozzarella, 50 g grated Parmesan cheese, 1 cup tomato purée, chilli pepper, extra-virgin olive oil.

In a small saucepan, sauté the thinly-sliced onion lightly in a little oil, then add the tomato purée and a pinch of salt, and leave to reduce for 20 minutes. In the meantime, cook the eggs

in a small oiled roasting-tin in a moderate oven. When the pasta is cooked, drain while it is still *al dente* and pour over the tomato sauce and the grated Parmesan. Spread in an oiled oven-proof dish, cover with the diced mozzarella and the eggs, sprinkle with a little chilli, and pop into the oven or under the grill for a few minutes until the mozzarella has melted. Remove from the oven, and serve.

LAMB SAUCE

◆

200 g lamb, 2 cloves garlic, 1 sprig rosemary, 2 bay leaves, 400 g tomato pulp, red wine, grated Pecorino cheese, extra-virgin olive oil, salt, pepper.

Cut the lamb into small pieces and sauté in a saucepan in plenty of oil along with the garlic cloves (which you should remove as soon as they colour), the rosemary and the bay leaves. Pour over a little wine, and let it evaporate. Then add the tomato pulp, season with salt and pepper and finish cooking over a low heat.
When the pasta is cooked, drain, and tip it into the sauce, mixing well. Finish off with a sprinkle of grated Pecorino cheese.

MUSHROOM AND LEEK SAUCE

◆

500 g fresh mushrooms, 2 leeks, 1 bay-leaf, 1 clove, 1 bunch parsley, extra-virgin olive oil, salt, pepper.

Clean the vegetables, removing the earthy residue from the mushrooms with a damp cloth. Slice both mushrooms and leeks and put them into a saucepan with a few dessertspoons of

oil, the bay leaf, the clove and a pinch of salt. Cover the pan, and leave to stew slowly over a low heat, adding a little salted hot water or stock from time to time if necessary. Just before you switch off the heat, season with freshly-ground pepper and sprinkle with finely-chopped parsley.

PEAS AND CRESCENZA CHEESE SAUCE

◆

250 g freshly podded peas, 2 small onions, 1 bunch parsley, 150 g Crescenza cheese, 30 g grated Parmesan cheese, 4 dessertspoons cream, extra-virgin olive oil, salt, pepper.

Clean and chop the onions and sauté them gently in a saucepan with a few dessertspoons of oil, then add the peas, season with salt and pepper and pour over half a glass of hot water. Cover, and continue cooking over a moderate heat for about 20 minutes, stirring every so often.
In the meantime, in a bowl mix the Crescenza with the cream, the chopped parsley and the grated Parmesan, beating together until you have a smooth creamy mixture. Add the cheese cream to the peas as soon as they are cooked and, stirring all the time, let the cheeses melt over a very low heat before using the sauce over short-cut pasta shapes.

OYSTER SAUCE

◆

16 oysters, 12 scallops, 1 shallot, 1/2 glass champagne, 60 g butter, salt, white pepper.

Open the oysters, clean them and extract the flesh, working over a container so that you can collect the water contained inside, which you should then sieve. Shell and trim the scallops, discarding the inedible parts and retaining only the white flesh and the coral roe.
In a saucepan, soften the finely-chopped shallot in the butter, and immediately pour over the champagne; let the flavours merge for a few minutes, then add the scallops, removing them after a few minutes with a slatted spoon.
Stir the sauce thoroughly, dilute with the oyster water, and when it is nice and hot again tip in the oysters and reheat the scallops in it too for a few minutes. Adjust salt to taste and season with a twist of freshly-ground white pepper, leaving the flavours to blend for a few minutes before use.

TUNA SAUCE ALL'ARRABBIATA

◆

150 g tuna in oil, 2 salted anchovies, 500 g tomato purée, 50 g black olives, 1 dessertspoon capers, 2 cloves garlic, 1 handful basil leaves, 1 pinch thyme, extra-virgin olive oil, chilli pepper, salt.

Break up the tuna with a fork and sauté it in a saucepan in a little oil. Then add the tomato purée and a little crumbled chilli. Flavour with thyme, and leave the sauce to reduce. Rinse the salt off the anchovies and remove any bones, then chop them with the capers. When the sauce is cooked, tip them in along with the pounded basil and garlic and the olives. Leave the flavours to blend and adjust salt to taste before switching off.

MULLET SAUCE

◆

300 g mullet fillets, 3 ripe firm tomatoes, 2 cloves garlic, ginger, 1 bunch parsley, 1/2 glass dry white wine, extra-virgin olive oil, salt.

In a saucepan, flavour a few dessertspoons of oil with the clove of garlic. As soon as the garlic begins to colour, remove it and drop in the mullet chopped into pieces and the ginger and sauté. Plunge the tomatoes in boiling water, then peel, seed and chop them and add them to the fish when the wine has almost completely evaporated. Adjust salt to taste and cook for 15 minutes, and complete with a sprinkle of chopped parsley.

CLAM AND TOMATO SAUCE

◆

500 g clams, 5 anchovies, 600 g ripe firm tomatoes, 3 cloves of garlic, a few basil leaves, 1/2 glass dry white wine, extra-virgin olive oil, red chilli pepper, salt.

Steep the clams in salted water for at least half an hour, then rinse them carefully. Place a large frying-pan on the heat, put in the clams and pour over the wine. When they open with the heat, drain and shell them. Sieve the cooking juices well and set aside. Clean and fillet the anchovies then, in a saucepan, stir them in hot oil with the crumbled chilli until they disintegrate. Plunge the tomatoes in boiling water, then peel, seed and chop them, and add them to the sauce along with the clams' cooking juices. Season with salt and leave the sauce to reduce. When the sauce is cooked, add the clams and the finely-chopped garlic and basil.

153

ZUCCHINI SAUCE

◆

3 zucchini, 1 bunch parsley or a few mint leaves, 1 clove garlic, grated hard ricotta cheese, extra-virgin olive oil, chilli pepper, salt.

Wash the zucchini and slice them thinly. In a non-stick saucepan heat a few dessertspoons of olive oil, tip in the zucchini and brown them evenly. When they are almost cooked, add salt and a pinch of chilli pepper, the sliced garlic and

the finely-chopped parsley. Drain the pasta (long shapes are recommended with this sauce) while it is still *al dente* and mix it with the zucchini sauce, adding a dash of fresh oil, and a sprinkle of grated ricotta.

154

ZUCCHINI AND PEA SAUCE

◆

4 zucchini, 250 g freshly podded peas, 2 leeks, 1 bunch parsley, basil, 3 dessertspoons cream, extra-virgin olive oil, salt, pepper.

Slice the leeks and sauté them in a saucepan in a few dessertspoons of oil, adding the peas before the leeks begin to brown. Wash, dry and slice the zucchini not too thinly, and stir them into the sauce after about 5 minutes. Leave the flavours to blend, then lower the heat, season with salt and a grind of fresh pepper, cover the pan and continue cooking for about 30 minutes. Mix well and, if necessary, add a little hot stock or water from time to time. When cooking is completed, sprinkle with chopped parsley and a few roughly-torn basil leaves, add the cream, and heat through thoroughly before switching off.

COLD AVOCADO SAUCE

◆

2 ripe avocados, the juice of 2 lemons, 2 cloves garlic, basil, coriander, 1 glass extra-virgin olive oil, red chilli pepper, salt.

Peel the avocados and cut the flesh into pieces, then whiz it in the blender with the garlic, the oil, the sieved lemon juice, a few leaves of basil, a pinch of coriander, one of salt and one of chilli pepper. The sauce is now ready to be served with the pasta of your choice.

COLD ROCKET SAUCE

◆

1 bunch rocket, 75 g grated Parmesan cheese, 75 g fresh soft cheese (ricotta, caprino etc.), 2.5 dl cream, salt, pepper.

In a bowl, blend the cheeses with the cream, seasoning with salt and a grind of pepper, until you have a smooth cream. Add the roughly-chopped rocket, diluting the mixture if it is too stiff with a few spoonfuls of the pasta cooking water.
Remember that if you use wild rocket you should use less since it has a much stronger flavour than the cultivated variety. You are also recommended to gather it in areas not subject to atmospheric pollution.

CONTENTS

156

INTRODUCTION

PASTA WITH MEAT

PASTA WITH FISH

PASTA WITH VEGETABLES, CHEESE, WINE…

BAKED PASTA

157

159

Printing completed in the month of July 2000
by Giunti Industrie Grafiche - Prato, Italy